ABRAHAM LINCOLN'S CONVENTION:

Chicago 1860

Also by Kenneth D. Ackerman

BOSS TWEED: *The Corrupt Pol who Conceived the Soul of Modern New York*

DARK HOUSE: *The Surprise Election and Political Murder of President James A. Garfield*

THE GOLD RING: *Jim Fisk, Jay Gould, and Black Friday, 1869*

YOUNG J. EDGAR: *Hoover and the Red care, 1919-1920*

ABRAHAM LINCOLN'S CONVENTION

Chicago 1860

The First Reports-

Compiled and presented by

Kenneth D. Ackerman

Viral History Press LLC
Falls Church, Virginia

ABRAHAM LINCOLN'S CONVENTION
Chicago 1860

Viral History Press LLC
Falls Church, Virginia

www.ViralHistoryPress.com

Library of Congress Cataloging-in-Publication data is available.

ISBN: 978-1-61945-019-6

Cover design by Paula Reichwald, Iossi.com

Contents:

PROLOGUE:

By Kenneth D. Ackerman

On May 16, 1860, with Civil War looming and the country torn by sectional hatreds over slavery, states rights, and clashing visions of the American future, the recently-formed Republican Party met in Chicago, Illinois, to choose its nominee for President. Looking back, its selection of Abraham Lincoln, a principled man uniquely qualified to lead the nation through the turmoil of disunion, war, and emancipation, seemed pre-ordained. Could it have been any other way? The country needed a special leader for a dangerous time, and one emerged. The nomination assured Lincoln's election. That November, Lincoln would face a crippled Democratic Party and win the Presidency with thirty-nine percent of the popular vote. Today, he tops almost every poll of historians and non-historians alike as the nation's single greatest and most admired president.

But Lincoln's nomination was no sure thing. In fact, almost until the minute it happened, it seemed far-fetched.

Lincoln was so obscure in May 1860 that, after his selection, major newspapers misspelled his name -- Abram instead of Abraham – and struggled to learn his background. The _New-York Times_, for one, described him as a "youngster who, with ragged trousers, used barefoot to drive his father's oxen and spend his days in splitting rails."

Every president is shaped by the nominating convention that chooses him to run. Lincoln's in 1860 not only was one of the most important, but also the most exciting ever in America up to that point. In a three day, three-ballot carnival of music, fireworks, and politics drawing some 40,000 people, it saw Lincoln and his friends outwit the leading celebrities of their party, capturing the prize with nerve, ambition, and brass tacks. They played the kind of hardball politics that usually made reformers cringe. Still, it gave us the best candidate anyone could have hoped for to save the country.

How? By all appearances, the Republican presidential nomination in 1860 had been locked up in advance by another candidate: William Seward, New York's distinguished U.S. Senator and former governor, backed by New York money, eastern abolitionists, and veteran political fixer Thurlow Weed, publisher of the influential _Albany Evening Journal_. Seward had launched a coordinated, well-funded national campaign. His managers in Chicago charmed delegates with champagne and oysters as their army of noisy boosters and clackers – imported by the trainload from New York's rowdy neighborhoods -- paraded through Chicago behind brass bands and colorful banners. Seward's committed delegates on the convention floor outnumbered those of every other candidate, though not quite an outright majority.

Should Seward stumble, a line of major figures stood ready to collect the prize: Ohio's Governor and former U.S. Senator Salmon P. Chase, Pennsylvania's Senator Simon Cameron, Missouri's Edward Bates, among others. Each had his own block of delegates, a national reputation, and plenty of friends.

Abraham Lincoln, by contrast, was a relative unknown. At 51 years old, he had held national office only once, serving a single term in the U.S. Congress in the late 1840s. He'd left his seat in 1848 after speaking out against the popular Mexican War. He'd twice failed to win an Illinois seat in the U.S. Senate. His 1858 debates with Democrat Stephen A. Douglas had won him national attention and a majority of the popular votes, but the Democratic-controlled state legislature that year still gave the seat to Douglas. (Prior to 1913, when the Seventeenth Amendment to the Constitution was ratified, U.S. Senators were chosen by state legislatures rather than by voters.) A self-educated lawyer, Lincoln had never managed a large company, never run a government agency, and had few backers outside his home state. An engaging public speaker, he suffered bouts of melancholy, stood awkwardly tall, and had a homely appearance. "If I had two faces," he once joked, "do you think this is the one I'd be wearing?"

In the end, "Honest Abe" and his operators captured the nomination by a host of tricks that made peoples' heads spin. Among other things, they pushed Republicans to hold their convention in Chicago, far from East Coast pressures, where they could use their local advantage to manipulate convention arrangements and pack the hall with Lincoln men. They forced a "unit rule" on Illinois's own twenty-two delegates, a tactic future Republican conventions would outlaw as an undemocratic tool for Bosses. They recast Lincoln's image from sharp railroad lawyer to folksy "rail splitter," though Lincoln hadn't done physical labor in decades. They cut deals for votes and launched whispering campaigns against rival candidates, calling them unelectable or worse.

Issues

Passions over of slavery and states rights had reached a boiling point in early 1860. The Missouri Compromise, which had papered over differences since 1820 by limiting slavery to

Southern states, had unraveled in 1854 with passage of the Kansas-Nebraska Act that suddenly permitted slavery into the free western territories. Then, in 1856, the Supreme Court upheld the Fugitive Slave law in its _Dred Scott v. Sandford_ decision, making slavery legal nationwide. The issue erupted in open violence in "Bloody Kansas," followed by John Brown's 1859 raid on Harper's Ferry, Virginia. President James Buchanan sat helplessly in the White House, unable or unwilling to staunch the crisis.

Most white Northerners abhorred slavery, despite personal prejudices against African Americans. They saw Southerners as bold and arrogant, dominating the economy with their huge plantations that inevitably threatened free farmers and factory workers up north. William H. Seward in 1858, as a United States Senator, predicted an "irrepressible conflict" between North and South. Lincoln too warned that the nation could not survive half slave, half free. Northerners and Southerners alike saw 1860 as a watershed. The choice of a next president would tip the balance, making the country unlivable for one side or the other.

By the time Republicans gathered in Chicago to pick a candidate, they had already seen the Democratic Party disintegrate over the issue. Democrats had met in Charleston, South Carolina, in late April but had disbanded their convention after 57 ballots without a nominee. Illinois U.S. Senator Stephen A. Douglas -- a champion of letting settlers decide for themselves whether to allow slavery through what he called "popular sovereignty" -- far outpolled his more dogmatic rivals, but he failed to satisfy the Party's rule requiring a two-thirds majority for nominees, a device designed to give slave states a veto. Delegates from seven southern states had stormed out after failing to break the impasse. Later that summer, the Democratic Party would split in two. Northerners, meeting in Baltimore, would nominate Douglas. Southerners would meet in Richmond, Virginia, future capitol of the Confederacy, and choose Kentuckian John Breckenridge, the country's sitting Vice President and a pro-slavery Southerner.

This split among Democrats already had spawned the creation of yet another new political force, the Constitutional Union Party. Shunning both Democrats and Republicans as sectional zealots, it met in Baltimore on May 9 to choose its own separate candidate for president, Tennessee U.S. Senator John Bell. Bell, a former Speaker of the House who owned 166 slaves, saw himself as a unifying force who could bridge North and South and avoid Civil War. To demonstrate his commitment to national harmony, he chose as his vice presidential running mate the prominent Massachusetts

Abraham Lincoln's Convention:

orator and former U.S. Senator Edward Everett – who later would give the main speech before Lincoln's own famous 1863 Gettysburg Address.

Chicago

As a result, Republicans, their Party just five years old, suddenly found themselves in a surprising position. As they gathered in Chicago in May 1860, filled its hotels and enjoyed the excitement, the delegates and politicos all recognized that whoever they chose as a candidate – unless they chose badly – could probably win the White House.

Following tradition, the candidates themselves stayed away -- Lincoln in Springfield and Seward in upstate New York -- as their "friends" set up shop in hotels around the convention hall to plead their cases. Nine slave states decided to boycott the convention (Alabama, Arkansas, Florida, Georgia, Louisiana, Mississippi, Tennessee, and the Carolinas).

All the delegates were chosen by state and/or local party meetings -- conventions and caucuses. Many were hand picked by local strongmen. *Primary elections giving voters a voice in party nominations would not exist until the Twentieth Century.* Practical politicians would make the choice, plying their craft on the loftiest stage of the era, their party's national convention.

Chicago itself in 1860 was a rugged frontier town of 100,000 on the banks of Lake Michigan, the fastest growing city in America. Visitors saw it as a place of contrasts, glaring wealth and poverty, luxury homes and mud streets, theaters and brothels. Growing rich from railroads and factories, the city sported forty large hotels, thousands of smokestacks, and a dozen baseball teams.

For the Republican Convention, Chicago built what was then the largest indoor arena in America. The "Wigwam," named for the large tents often erected for religious camp meetings, would hold twelve thousand people. It had space for 466 delegates on its wide stage, a standing area (no chairs) for spectators, and an upstairs gallery for ladies with escorts. Its twenty-foot doors could open and allow thousands more to peer in from outside on nearby Lake and Market streets. The stage itself was lit by gas lamps and decked with evergreen wreaths and large oil-painted figures representing Agriculture, Justice, Liberty, Mechanics and the Arts. Busts of prominent statesmen dotted the room along with coats of arms of the different States.

Some 40,000 strangers would invade Chicago for what would be the largest political gathering ever yet held in America. To greet them, the city lined its streets in red, white, and blue bunting, posted flags and banners, and provided fire works, booming cannons, and marching brass bands. Railroads provided special trains for delegates traveling from New York and other east coast cities, with crowds and marching bands to greet them at stops along the way.

It would be a grand old time, no matter what.

The Newspapers

In this *History Short*, we tell the story of Lincoln's nominating convention primarily through the eyes of newspaper writers – giving it the immediacy and excitement of the moment. Newspapers dominated the American media in 1860 and they covered politics intensely. Cutting edge technologies were changing the face of news at that point: the telegraph, which allowed stories to flash across the country almost instantly from the touch of an operator's key; huge steam presses that could produce tens of thousands of copies in a few hours; and type-setting machines that allowed quick assembly of multiple daily editions. Lincoln's convention in 1860 would be the first with telegraph instruments wired to transmit news directly from the convention floor. The Chicago Wigwam itself made room for at least sixty reporters to cover the story from the scene.

The *New York Herald* and *New York Sun* had the biggest circulations in 1860, selling 77,000 and 60,000 copies each day, respectively. But the closest to being a truly national platform was the *New York Tribune*, still operating under its founding publisher and editor, Horace Greeley. In additional to its 55,000 daily circulation in 1860, the *Tribune* also produced a weekly edition with over 100,000 copies mailed across the country and passed hand to hand or shared by friends in small towns. Its actual readership was estimated at half a million. Frontier Illinois alone received 10,000 copies each week, making Greeley perhaps the best-known "pundit" of the era.

Greeley would play a uniquely large role in shaping American journalism in the 1800s. Eccentric, talkative, disheveled, with an unmistakable wispy beard, he would take credit for training an entire generation of editors, writers, and craftsman at the *Tribune* who would lead American newspapers for the next thirty years: Charles Dana at the *New York Sun*, Henry Raymond and George Jones at *The New-York*

Times, Whitelaw Reid at the *Tribune*, George W. Curtis at *Harper's Weekly*, among others.

Most newspapers in 1860 were owned, controlled by, or allied with political parties. Independence was rare, and newsmen saw no conflict in openly taking sides. Both Greeley and Henry Raymond, publisher of *The New-York Times*, sat as delegates at Lincoln's 1860 nominating convention. Greeley had been a member of Congress in the 1840s. Raymond had been New York Lieutenant Governor and speaker of the state assembly, and would be elected to Congress in 1865. Thurlow Weed, the acknowledged leader of the Seward campaign, published the *Albany Evening Journal*, and Lincoln backer Joseph Medill ran the *Chicago Tribune*.

Here, too, Greeley had been the trail-blazer, having helped conceive the "Tippicanoe and Tyler Too" campaign for Whig nominee William Henry Harrison in 1840 and made his *New York Tribune* a campaign headquarters for Republican John Fremont in 1856. In 1872, Greeley would run for president himself, winning the nominations of both the Democratic and the Liberal Republican parties, though losing in a landslide to the incumbent, Ulysses S. Grant.

In 1860, Greeley came to Chicago with the singular purpose of wanting to stop William Seward from winning the nomination. Greeley had once been close friends with

Seward, a fellow New York progressive, but they had broken years earlier in argument over a patronage job. Now, ostracized by New York's pro-Seward delegation, Greeley attended the Convention as a carpetbag delegate from Oregon and campaign loudly for Missouri's Edward Bates.

In this *History Short*, we use the daily reporting of Greeley's *New York Tribune* as the main source for coverage of the convention's daily proceedings – just as did the half million daily and weekly readers of the *Tribune* at the time. By-lines were rare in 1860s newspapers, so many of the fine journalists behind the columns remain anonymous.

For commentary, we turn to one of the most flamboyant newsmen of the era, Joe Howard Jr. of *The New-York Times*. Born in Brooklyn in 1833, graduate of the Troy Polytechnic Institute (today's RPI), Howard gave up a career in civil engineering to join the *Times* in early 1860 to cover a shoemakers strike in Lynn, Massachusetts. His dogged reporting sometimes crossed the ethical line even by Nineteenth Century standards. During the Civil War, he covered dozens of battles from Bull Run to Balls Bluff, but was also caught violating military orders by sneaking into the funeral of General Philip Kearney – killed in action at the Second Battle of Manassas/Bull Run -- to snoop on celebrities.

Abraham Lincoln's Convention:

Most notoriously, Howard was prosecuted in May 1864 and spent fourteen weeks in a military prison for producing a fake story claiming that President Lincoln planned to draft some 400,000 additional soldiers to bolster General Grant's army in Virginia. The episode came just a few months after the New York City draft riots and terrified many New Yorkers. Howard later admitted that he had designed the story to aid certain Wall Street speculators placing bets on the New York Gold Exchange.

Still, Howard's reporting on the 1860 presidential race was first rate, earning him a national following and a rare by-line. After the war, Howard would become one of the best-known writers in America, long-time president of the New York Press Club, and author of a syndicated column in addition to editing the _Brooklyn Eagle_ and other local papers.

Finally, for context, we include a smattering of eye-witness accounts, letters, interviews and memoir excerpts from key players. For ease of reading, we have made minor edits, added annotations and background, and updated formatting. Otherwise, we have left the original text alone. We hope you enjoy it, a good story told well by talented people who saw it with their own eyes.

We give special thanks for help in preparing this _History Short_ to the staff at the Library of Congress in

Washington, D.C., a true national treasure that gave us easy access to all original material. Unless otherwise noted, they are the source of everything you see here. Thanks also to my friends and colleagues Steve Terman and David O. Stewart for feedback on the concept, Linette Abraham Vann for help in preparing the manuscript, and Paula Reichwald of Igossi.Com for designing the cover and converting the book into digital form.

See the full official proceedings of the 1860 Convention online at the University of California Digital Library, http://archive.org/details/proceedingsofrep00repuiala

1. HEADLINE: THEY NOMINATED *WHO*?

The New-York Times, Saturday, May 19, 1860.
By Joe Howard, Jr.

FROM CHICAGO.

THE REPUBLICAN TICKET FOR 1860.

Abram Lincoln, of Illinois, Nominated For President.

_____

The Late Senatorial Contest in Illinois to be Re-Fought on a Wider Field.

Disappointment of the Friends of Mr. Seward

INTENSE EXCITEMENT AND ENTHUSIASM

Special Dispatch to the New-York Times
Chicago, Friday, May 18

The work of the Convention is ended. The youngster who, with raged trousers, used barefoot to drive his father's oxen and spend his days in splitting rails, has risen to high eminence, and ABRAM LINCOLN, of Illinois, is declared its candidate for President by the National Republican Party.

The result was effected by the change of votes in the Pennsylvania, New-Jersey, Vermont, and Massachusetts delegations.

Mr. SEWARD's friends assert indignantly, and with a great deal of feeling, that they were grossly deceived and betrayed. The recusanis endeavored to mollify New-York by offering her the Vice-Presidency, and agreeing to support any man she might name, but they declined the position, though they remain firm in the ranks, having moved to make Lincoln's nomination unanimous. Mr. Seward's friends feel greatly chagrined and disappointed. [Recunasi is an old word referring to English Roman Catholics in the 1600s who rejected the Church of England, a crime back then.]

Western pride is gratified by the nomination, which plainly indicated the departure of political supremacy from the Atlantic States. ...

Immense enthusiasm exists, and everything here would seem to indicate a spirited and successful canvass. The city is alive with processions, meetings, music, and noisy demonstrations. One hundred guns were fired this evening.

The Convention was the most enthusiastic ever known in the country, and if one were to judge from appearances here, the ticket will sweep the country

Great inquiry has been made this afternoon into the history of Mr. Lincoln. The only evidence that he has a history as yet discovered, is that he had a stump canvass with Mr. Douglas, in which he was beaten. [U.S. Senator Stephen A. Douglas from Illinois was the likely Democratic nominee and Lincoln's likely chief opponent for President. Lincoln actually had won the popular vote in his 1858 Senate contest against Douglas, but the Democratic Illinois legislature nevertheless awarded the seat to Douglas.] *He is not very strong at the west, but is unassailable in his private character.*

Many of the delegates went home this evening by the 9 o'clock train. Others leave in the morning.....

Massachusetts delegates, with their brass band, are parading the streets, calling at the various headquarters of the other delegations, serenading and bidding them farewell. "Hurrah for Lincoln and Hamlin – Illinois and Maine!!" is the universal shout, and the sympathy for the bottom dog is the all-pervading sentiment.

The "Wide-Awakes," numbering about two thousand men, accompanied by thousands of citizens, have a grand torch-light procession. The German Republican Club has another. The office of the Press and Tribune *[today's* Chicago Tribune*] is brilliantly illuminated, and has a large transparency over the door saying "For President, Honest Old Abe." A bonfire thirty feet in circumference burns in front of the Tremont House, where thirty-three guns were fired from the top, and illumines the city for miles around. The city is one blaze of illumination. Hotels, stores and private residences, shining with hundreds of patriotic dips. Enough.*

--Howard

2. THE CANDIDATE: ABRAHAM LICOLN

Lincoln launched his formal bid for the presidency in 1860 at the Illinois state party convention in Decatur on May 9, just one week before the national gathering in Chicago. Here, his friends anointed him "the rail-splitter candidate," a common-man image borrowed from Andrew Jackson's "Old Hickory" and William Henry Harrison's "Hard Cider and Log Cabin." Lincoln saw weakness in the other contenders: Seward too extreme, Chase too stiff, Cameron too corrupt, Bates too old. His strategy at the Chicago Convention would be simple: prevent Seward, the favorite, from sweeping the hall on the first ballot, and position himself, Lincoln, to emerge the winner in the later voting.

Lincoln had withdrawn from politics after leaving his Congressional seat in 1849, but felt compelled to jump back in when Congress passed the 1854 Kansas-Nebraska Act that opened the door to slavery in the free territories. Lincoln spoke out against the Act and, by 1856, had made an impression. He received 110 votes for Vice President at that year's first-ever Republican national convention.

Lincoln next decided to challenge Democrat Stephen A. Douglas for the Illinois U.S. Senate seat in 1858. He debated Douglas twelve times and outpolled Douglas 190,000 to 176,000 in popular votes, despite Douglas's being awarded the seat. Eastern big-city newspapers carried transcripts of the Lincoln-Douglas debates, and Lincoln began speaking around the country. He travelled to Ohio and Indiana and finally won an invitation to speak at New York City's Cooper Union in February 1860. By the time Lincoln returned home to Illinois, he had won a following.

Still, he played coy, and even close friends like Illinois U.S. Senator Lyman Trumbull considered his plan far-fetched.

Letter to Abraham Lincoln from Lyman Trumbull (United States Senator from Illinois)

April 24, 1860. Washington, D. C.   Lincoln papers, Library of Congress

My Dear Sir,

I am going to write you candidly and frankly my impressions in regard to the Presidency, for such I know is the way you would desire me to speak, & I shall hope in return to be put fully in possession of your views.

First in regard to yourself. I am inclined to believe as between you and Gov. Seward, if the contest should assume that shape, that he would most likely succeed. I will not go into a

calculation to show this, but I have talked the matter over with friends here and that seems to be the impression of those men, who do not want Seward nominated. When urging your claims, I am almost always met with the remark, "if you are going to nominate a man of that stamp, why not take Seward." There seems to be a disposition in the public mind to associate you together, from the fact, I suppose, that you have both given expression to a similar sentiment in regard to the ultimate extinction of slavery. It matters not whether there is any foundation for this or not-- I am not arguing the matter, but simply stating what others say.

Second. Can Seward be elected if nominated? The impression here is among all except his own friends that he cannot. ...

Yours truly

Lyman Trumbull

———————

Letter to Lyman Trumbull from Abraham Lincoln

April 29, 1860. Springfield, Illinois.
Collected Works of Abraham Lincoln, Vol. IV, p. 46

My dear Sir:

Yours of the 24th. was duly received; and I have postponed answering it, hoping by the result at Charleston, to know who is to lead our adversaries, before writing. But Charleston hangs fire, and I wait no longer.

As you request, I will be entirely frank. The taste is in my mouth a little; and this, no doubt, disqualifies me, to some extent, to form correct opinions...

A word now for your own special benefit. You better write no letters which can possibly be distorted into opposition, or quasi opposition to me. There are men on the constant watch for such things out of which to prejudice my peculiar friends against you. While I have no more suspicion of you than I have of my best friend living, I am kept in a constant struggle against suggestions of this sort. I have hesitated some to write this paragraph, lest you should suspect I do it for my own benefit, and not for yours; but on reflection I conclude you will not suspect me.

Let no eye but your own see this---not that there is anything wrong, or even ungenerous, in it; but it would be misconstrued. Your friend as ever A. LINCOLN

The Illinois Republican party held its state convention in Decatur on May 9, 1860, one week before the national convention in Chicago. One of the delegates in Decatur was a young lawyer from nearby Danville named Joseph G. Cannon. Cannon would become a U.S. congressman in 1873, serve fifty years in the House, and become Speaker from 1903 to 1911. Here is his account of how Lincoln launched his presidential campaign:

Interview with Joseph G. Cannon when he was Speaker of the House, published in the *World's Work*, February 1907.

"I FIRST MET MR. LINCOLN IN MAY, 1860," SAID SPEAKER Cannon, as he chewed the end of a long, black cigar. "A farmer by the name of Hackett hitched up a two-horse wagon and loaded a lot of us young fellows into it. There was an old fellow by the name of Vanderen, who kept a little two-story hotel at Tuscola, Illinois, from which place we started, and he drove across the prairie with us to Decatur. When we entered the place and drove along the principal street, we saw Lincoln standing on the sidewalk in front of the hotel. Vanderen spied him because he had lived in Springfield and knew Lincoln by sight. Vanderen said, 'There's Abe!' He yelled out, 'Howdy, Abe!' Lincoln's head went up and he answered, 'Howdy, Arch!'

"A little later, we went down to the railroad station and there saw Lincoln writing a telegram. You know, this was at the time of the Illinois State Convention, held to name delegates to the National Convention that nominated Lincoln for the Presidency. One of the boys who was with us, and who knew Mr. Lincoln, stepped up beside him and began to ask him about his candidacy for the Presidential nomination. Everybody in Illinois and all over the country had got to talking about Abe Lincoln, so it was no secret. Lincoln looked at his questioner and in that drawl of his said: 'I'm most too much of a candidate to be here and

not enough of one to stay away!'

"This was the day before the convention. Decatur was a place of seven or eight thousand people and every house in the town had been occupied long before we got there. We had to camp out with our wagon in an empty lot as best we could. I can see that convention hall yet. They made it by setting a row of good-sized saplings upright in the ground and then putting up another row opposite them. Scantlings were put across near the top and the whole thing was covered over with green branches for a roof. Rough boards were placed on short pieces of tree-trunk and these formed seats for delegates and onlookers. The whole thing was in the shape of an amphitheatre, and plenty big enough to accommodate everybody.

"The convention assembled, as I recollect it, at 10:30 o'clock in the morning. Lincoln's name was in every mouth and in those stirring times everything was on fire. There was a Chicago contingent, and a few others here and there, who were for Seward, but they were so completely in the minority that not much attention was paid to them. The convention was called to order and after the prayer a cry was started on the platform: 'Open a passage way! Open a passage way! Let John Hanks and Dick Oglesby through! They have some rails that John Hanks and Abe Lincoln made in 1830.'

"They came in with the rails, which had a piece of cotton cloth rolled round them. When this cloth was unrolled it disclosed the legend: 'These rails were made by John Hanks and Abraham Lincoln in 1830.'

They were walnut rails, such as would be hard to find now, but there was plenty of that kind of fine hard wood in those days. The crowd went wild and it was some time before order was restored.

"There was a yell for Lincoln. After a bit, he appeared on the outskirts of the crowd. By this time the crowd was very dense and somebody yelled 'Mr. Lincoln is here!' Then everybody began to holler: 'Bring him down to the platform!' Lincoln was a mighty long man, but they carried him down over their heads right over everybody in the crowd. I have heard of that sort of thing, but never before nor since have I seen a long fellow like Lincoln passed hand over hand over a solid mass of people. As they passed him along, everybody shouted, 'Speech! speech!'

"Lincoln smiled and bowed. After thanking them, he said that he would not delay the business of the convention, as it was a busy time of the year for the people of Illinois. At this stage of the proceeding, some fellow yelled out: 'Abe, did you split them rails?' Said he: 'John Hanks says I split those rails. I don't know whether I did or not, but I have made many a better one!' Then the crowd yelled. That is substantially all I saw of Lincoln at that time at Decatur. He had a splendid tenor voice, as I remember it, one that would carry to the utmost limits of a vast crowd.

"I felt well acquainted with Lincoln when I was practicing law in those days in the old Eighth Illinois Circuit. Everybody knew him or about him, and almost everybody was fond of talking about him. ... Almost all of the people I met in those days knew him, some on sight, and some personally. I was lawyer for a good many of those folks and

they would delight in telling me how he urged this case or argued that one, or of some story he told them. He surely was a great favorite...."

To manage his campaign at the national convention in Chicago, Lincoln chose two of his oldest and closest friends in Illinois politics. One was Norman Judd, a Chicago railroad lawyer who had served with Lincoln in the Illinois legislature and now chaired of the Illinois State Republican Committee. The other was David Davis, a state circuit judge who also had served with Lincoln in the Illinois legislature and presided as judge in the same circuit where Lincoln pled cases. Davis had managed Lincoln's earlier unsuccessful bid for the Illinois U.S. Senate seat in 1858, and now would be Lincoln's chief strategist and advocate in Chicago.

Interview with Normal Judd, February 28, 1876.
From *An Oral History of Abraham Lincoln*,
Edited by Michael Burlingame

"After the Decatur Convention in 1860 Lincoln came to me [and] we talked over the matter of appointing delegates to Chicago. I told him I had no influence in that Convention, but that if he had any desires in relation to the matter I would do my best to have them brought about. He then told me that he wished but one thing, and that was that Judge [David] Davis should be sent as one of the delegates. And, he added, 'Judd, you ought to

go.'....

"When we came to get the Chicago Wigwam ready to be occupied by the convention I superintended the arrangements of the seats for the delegates on the stage. I put New York about the centre on the right hand side and grouped New England, Wisconsin, Minnesota, and all the strong Seward States immediately around her.

"On the other side I put Illinois Pennsylvania and Indiana, and Missouri, and grouped around these the delegates from the border states, and all the small doubtful delegations.

"The advantage of the arrangement was, that when the active excitement and canvassing in the Convention came on, the Seward men couldn't get over among the doubtful delegations at all to log-roll with them, being absolutely hemmed in by their own followers who were not likely to be swerved from their set preference for Seward, &c &c."

3. THE FRONT-RUNNER: WILLIAM H. SEWARD

Seward, the front-runner, had distinguished himself over thirty years in New York State politics by constantly taking progressive stands on burning social issues. As governor, he backed immigrants and Catholics, allowing them to teach in New York public schools. He championed prison reforms and fought corruption in state government. But most of all, he opposed slavery (which was not fully abolished in New York State until 1827). As governor, he protected runaway slaves entering the state and, later, as a U.S. Senator, he told one crowd that slavery "must be abolished, and you and I must do it."

Seward frightened moderates who hoped to keep peace with the slave-holding South. Going into the 1860 presidential contest, many considered him unelectable. Still, Seward had more support and more delegates on route to Chicago than any other candidate.

To lead his campaign in Chicago, Seward too chose one of his oldest and closest friends in politics: Thurlow Weed, publisher of the *Albany Evening Journal*. Weed had helped engineer nominations and elections of presidents from William Henry Harrison in 1840 to Zachary Taylor in 1848 and several in between. As Seward stayed home in upstate Auburn, New York, Weed came early to Chicago to start working the delegates behind the scenes.

> From P. Orman Ray, professor at Northwestern University after the Civil War, who in 1916 compiled this description of Weed's operation from eye witnesses and presented it as an address to the Chicago Historical Society titled <u>The Convention That Nominated Lincoln</u>:

As early as Saturday evening... Thurlow Weed also arrived in Chicago, Seward's campaign manager, the first Republican boss of New York State and the ablest political tactician that had appeared in American politics up to that time. Governor Morgan made the Tremont House his headquarters, while Weed established himself at the Richmond House...

Here Weed was later found by Carl Schurz, chairman of the Seward delegation from Wisconsin, surrounded not by political luminaries of the first magnitude, but by a crowd of satellites, some of whom did not strike Schurz as desirable companions of New York politicians-apparently men of the baser sort whom Weed had brought with him to aid in doing his work.

"What that work consisted in, *I* could guess," says Schurz, "from the conversations *I* was permitted to hear, for they talked very freely about the great services they had rendered or were going to render. They had marched, they had treated members of other delegations with no end of champagne and cigars, to win them for Seward, if not as their first, then at least as their second, choice, to be voted for on the second or third ballot. They had hinted to this man and that man supposed to wield some influence, that if he could throw that influence for Seward, he might, in case of success, count upon proper 'recognition.' They had spent money freely and let everybody understand that there was a great lot more to spend.

"Among these men Thurlow Weed moved as a great captain, with ceaseless activity and noiseless step, receiving their reports and giving new instructions in his peculiar whisper, now and then taking one into a corner of the room for secret talk, or disappearing with another through a side door for transactions still more secret"....

The character and behavior of the New York contingent of Seward "boosters" were subjects of more comment in the newspapers than was true of any other delegation. "The New Yorkers here," says one eyewitness, "are of a class unknown to the Western Republican politicians. They can drink more whiskey, swear as loud and long, sing as bad songs, and 'get up and howl' as ferociously as any crowd of Democrats you ever heard or heard of. They are opposed, as they say, to being 'too damned virtuous.' They hoot at the idea that Seward could not sweep all the northern states, and swear that he would have a party in every slave state in less than a year that would clean out the disunionists from shore to shore.

At night most of them who are not engaged in caucusing, are doing what ill-tutored youths call 'raising hell generally.' Wherever you find them, the New York politicians, of whatever party, are a peculiar party." The leader of these New York roustabouts, it may be interesting to add, was no less a distinguished personage than one Tom Hyer, "a noted bruiser" or prize fighter of that day.

Thurlow Weed, leader of the Seward campaign in Chicago.

4. EVE OF THE CONVENTION: POLITICS

The New-York Times, Wednesday, May 16, 1860.

By Joe Howard, Jr.

Immense Gathering of the Republicans.

The Bates and McLean Interests in the Background.

STRONG PARTIALITY FOR MR.

SEWARD.

Coalition of the Massachusetts, New-Jersey, Penn-Sylvania and Illinois Delegations.

COL. FREMONT A POSSIBLE CANDIDATE.

Special Dispatch to the New-York Times.
CHICAGO, Tuesday, May 15.

A great crowd of people arrived to-day by the morning and evening trains. The various delegations are full, and are busy *arranging their committee-men and officers.*

The city is thronged with strangers from all sections of the country, who expect by outside pressure to influence the action of the Convention. Probably no former Convention was so utterly "at sea" the day before organization as this one seems to be. The friends of each candidate press their choice with persistency and energy.

The several candidates, by their factors, have engaged spacious apartments, where at all hours of the day and night are found crowds of the faithful, who willingly drink and smoke at the expense of the host, and pay for their fare in outside talk and bluster.

The Seward men have the best organization, and the best workers. They do not flinch in their work, and while they do not for an instant show signs of discouragement, they are nevertheless affected by the tremendous opposition which they find to their candidate. They are urged by the friends of [rival candidate Edward] *BATES to give up their man and go for success.* [Edward Bates, 67 years old, a respected lawyer and state legislator from Missouri, claimed to represent the border states and presented himself to the Convention as a unifying moderate.]

To these representations they answer, that to give up Mr. SEWARD would be a shameful neglect of their proper standard-bearer, and also a backing down from principles for the sake of spoils, which they will not consent to; so they stand firm, but are compelled to acknowledge to themselves that the speck has become a cloud, and may yet be a storm, pregnant with disaster to themselves and ruin to

Abraham Lincoln's Convention:

the party. The fact that a majority of the Convention is in favor of
SEWARD no one denies; but it is also certain that a majority of the
Convention look fearfully to the election in case he is nominated.

There is no organized opposition. There are many factions,
each under ambitious leaders, each striving for individual success.
Prominent among these the Cameron, the Banks, the McLean, the
Chase, the Lincoln and Wade parties. [The candidates referred to
here were: Simon Cameron, Pennsylvania's U.S. Senator and
"favorite son" candidate for the nomination; Nathaniel Banks,
governor of Massachusetts; John McLean, 75 years old, a
sitting justice on the United States Supreme Court Justice who
had written a sharp dissent in the notorious 1857 Dred Scott v.
Sandford decision that upheld the Fugitive Slave Law; Salmon
P. Chase, Ohio governor and former Senator, popular as an
ardent abolitionist but whose stiff personality was off-putting
even to his own Ohio delegation; and Benjamin Wade, a U.S.
Senator from Ohio.]

The Pennsylvanians predict the utter ruin of
Republicanism in the event of SEWARD'S nomination, though they
admit he will run as well as any straight Republican.

The delegations of Pennsylvania, Illinois and New-Jersey,
called formally on the Massachusetts delegation this evening, and in
set speeches protested against the nomination of Mr. SEWARD. ....
Mr. KELLOGG, of Massachusetts, moved that each delegation present

the names which, in its opinion, were the best for the candidacy. This was agreed to. Pennsylvania offered CAMERON, BATES *and* MCLEAN. *Illinois named* LINCOLN, CAMERON *and* BANKS. *New-Jersey gave* [William L.] DAYTON, BANKS *and* LINCOLN *; thus playing into each other's hands in a very significant manner. The discussion which followed was a very excited one, and without coming to any definite result, the meeting was adjourned at a late hour.* [Dayton, a former U.S. Senator, was the Republican Party's nominee for Vice President in 1856. In 1860, he was acting as a place-holder "favorite son" for New Jersey.]

The Banks men feel elated that his name is invariably mentioned as one who stands a good chance in case Mr. SEWARD *is dropped. They claim that* SEWARD *will run as well on the second ballot as he will at any other time; that at the fourth he will be dropped and* BANKS' *stock rise.*

The general impression outside of the Seward ranks is, that if SEWARD *is dropped, an outsider will have to be taken up....*

The Michigan Central Railroad took the Massachusetts delegation and a few members of the Press, on an excursion to Hyde Park this afternoon, GILMORE'S *band furnished the music, and at a collation served at the hotel, strong Seward speeches were made, and a salute of thirty-three guns were fired in his honor.*

Mass meetings were held this evening in front of the Briggs House and the Richmond House.

Mr. [Horace] *Greeley has made a great sensation here. He is surrounded by a crowd wherever he goes, who besiege him for a speech, and failing in that, seduce him into a conversation, which inevitably becomes a speech ere he closes. Some foolish wag pinned to his coat tail a paper bearing the inscription, "For WM. H. SEWARD," and for several hours he unconsciously carried the irrepressible badge with him. .* [Greeley, a notorious publicity hound, was opposing New York's favorite son, Seward, and backing Edward Bates for the nomination.]

A large and enthusiastic assembly met at the Wigwam this evening, numbering at least five thousand people. They were addressed by Gen. NYE, Mr. CORWIN, and Mr. WOODFORD, of New-York. They hizzaed, cheered and sang so enthusiastically, and evinced so hearty an appreciation of the good things, that it was almost an impossibility to break up the meeting.

A very life-like picture of the late Senator BRODERICK occupies a conspicuous position in the Wigwam. It was loaned to the Convention by its owner, and the Committee wrote a letter of thanks in which they took occasion to refer to BRODERICK'S life, character, and achievements, in most honorable terms. [David C. Broderick, a United States Senator from California, had been shot and killed in September 1859 in a duel with the leader of a pro-slavery Democratic group there, making him a martyr among Republicans.]

The action of Virginia this afternoon, has caused quite a

flutter in all ranks. This delegation has, heretofore, been openly and boldly for Seward, but now promises that in case the vote becomes very close, Virginia will decline voting, and in that way damage him fifteen votes.

A new ticket is gaining some strength, LINCOLN and FESSESDEN being the candidates. FESSENDEN has been sent for, and will be here in the morning to manage his own case. [William Pitt Fessenden was the Republican U.S. Senator from Maine.]

At the various caucuses this evening, the delegations stood as follows :

Pennsylvania a unit for Gen. CAMERON,

New-York the same for Mr. SEWARD.

Wisconsin and Vermont for Mr. SEWARD.

Massachusetts divided between Messrs. SEWARD, BANKS and McLEAN. After a severe struggle, they determined to stand by Mr. SEWARD until it was evident he could not be nominated. They will cast a full complimentary vote for BANKS. ASHMUN is the leader of the Delegation.

Indiana is mostly for BATES.

Illinois is for LINCOLN.

Missouri goes for BATES.

Ohio is all split up. They pretend to regard SEWARD, BANKS and CHASE as dead, and that the struggle will be between WADE, CAMERON, LINCOLN and BATES.

The full choice of Pennsylvania is CAMERON and LINCOLN

Abraham Lincoln's Convention:

[FOR VICE PRESIDENT], *while the Illinois reverses the ticket.* LIN-
COLN'S *friends say that nothing save a high regard for the integrity
of the party can persuade him to accept the second position.*

*The streets of Chicago are alive with processions to-night.
There is a Lincoln procession headed by* GILMORE'S *Band, and a
Seward procession having the Light Guard Band. Thousands swell
them, attracted by the music, and the frequent orations delivered at
every corner. Banners are hung across the streets, with the name of*
LINCOLN *upon them, and the omnibus horses are gaily decorated
with Lincoln flags and Lincoln tokens.*

*The weather is delightful. The landlords are disposed to be
accommodating, but oh ! the accommodations!*   HOWARD.

Letter to Abraham Lincoln from Nathan M. Knapp, an Illinois delegate and
Lincoln ally at the Convention.

May 14, 1860 Chicago.   Lincoln papers, Library of Congress.

Dear Sir:

*Things are working; keep a good nerve -- be not surprised at any
result -- but I tell you that your chances are not the worst... We are
laboring to make you the second choice of all the Delegations we can
where we cannot make you first choice. We are dealing tenderly with
delegates, taking them in detail, and making no fuss. Be not too
Expectant but rely upon our discretion. Again I say brace your
nerves for any result. truly your friend*

N M Knapp

Letter to Abraham Lincoln from Charles H. Ray, an editor at the _Chicago Press and Tribune_ supporting Lincoln.

Chicago, May 14, 1860   Lincoln papers, Library of Congress.

Profoundly Private

My Dear Lincoln.

Your friends are at work for you hard, and with great success. Your show on the first ballot will not be confined to Illinois, and after that it will be strongly developed....

Don't be too sanguine. Matters now look well and as things stand to-day I had rather have your chances than those of any other man. But don't get excited.

Yours faithfully   C.H. Ray

Telegram to Abraham Lincoln from David Davis and Jesse K. Dubois, another Lincoln ally at the Convention.

May 15, 1860. Chicago, Illinois.   Lincoln papers, Library of Congress.
They are quiet but moving heaven & Earth. Nothing will beat us but old fogy politicians. The heart of the delegates are with us   Davis & Dubois

Judge David Davis, leader of the Lincoln forces at the convention.

5. MAY 16: DAY 1-
SPEECHES AND CEREMONY.

For the _New York Tribune_ reports on Convention proceedings, we have used below both the telegraphed Regular Reports sent immediately as events occurred as well as the fuller dispatches filed later in the day, interspersing them chronologically.

Drawing of the scene inside the Chicago Wigwam, from Harper's Weekly, May 1860.

From the *New York Tribune*
Thursday morning, May 17, 1860:

THE CHICAGO CONVENTION.

THE ORGANIZATION.

GEORGE ASHMUN OF MASSACHUSETTS PRESIDENT.

Mr. Seward's Prospects Brightening.

MR. LINCOLN CLOSE UPON HIM.

REGULAR REPORT OF THE PROCEEDINGS.

Chicago, Wednesday, May 16, 1860.

The Republican National convention assembled to-day at the "Wigwam."

The doors were opened at 11 o'clock.

Long before that hour the concourse of people assembled around the doors numbered many thousands more than could gain admittance to the building.

As soon as the doors were opened the entire body of Wigwam was solidly packed with men. The seats in the galleries were equally closely packed with ladies.

The interior of the hall was handsomely decorated with evergreen, statuary and flowers, and presented a striking appearance.

There were not less than ten thousand persons in the building, while the open doors displayed to view crowds in the streets unable to obtain more than a glimpse inside of the hall.

At 12 o'clock the Convention was called to order by Gov. [Edwin D.] *Morgan of New-York, Chairman of the National Committee, as follows:*

On the 22d of December last, the Republican National Committee, at a meeting convened for the purpose in the City of New-York, issued a call for a National Convention, which I will now read:

"A National Republican Convention will meet on Wednesday, the 16th day of May next at 12 o'clock for the nomination of candidates to be supported for President and Vice-President at the next election."

He then continued as follows:

"In compliance therewith, the people have sent representatives here to deliberate upon measures or carrying into effect the object of the call. . . ."

Gov. Morgan, at the conclusion of his remarks, then named the Hon. DAVID WILMOT of Penn. For temporary President. [Immense applause.] *Carried unanimous.* [Wilmot, a Pennsylvania congressman from 1845 through 1851, had made himself a Republican hero by authoring the Wilmot Proviso designed to ban slavery in land taken during the Mexican War. The House of Representatives twice passed Wilmot's ban, technically an amendment to the appropriation for the Mexican War, but the Senate rejected it each time. It became a rallying point for early Free Soil champions.]

The Chair named Judge Marshall of Md., and [former] *Gov.* [Chauncey Fitch] *Cleveland of Conn. to conduct Mr. Wilmot to his seat. Judge Marshall introduced Mr. Wilmot as the man who dared to do right regardless of consequence. With such a man there is no such word as fail.*

Mr. WILMOT addressed the Convention briefly, returning thanks for the high and undeserved honor. He would carry the remembrance of it with him to the day of his death. It was unnecessary for him to remind the Convention of the high duty devolved upon them. A great sectional interest had for years dominated with a high hand over the affairs of the country. It has bent all its energy on the extension and naturalization of Slavery. . . . . The Constitution was not ordained to embrace Slavery within all the limits of the country. The Founding Fathers lived and died in the faith that Slavery was a blot, and would soon be washed out. Had they deemed that the Revolution of 1776 was to establish a great slave empire, not one would have drawn the sword on such a cause. The battle was fought to establish freedom. Slavery is sectional –

Freedom is national. *[Applause.]* He deemed it necessary to remind the delegates of the outrages and usurpations of the Democratic party. . . . . The safety of the Free States requires the Republicans should take the Government and administer it as it has been administered by Washington, Jefferson, and Jackson even down to Van Buren and Polk. . . . He assumed his duties, exhorting a spirit of harmony to control the action of the delegates....

The Rev. Mr. HUMPHRY of Illinois then delivered the opening prayer.

Presentation of the Delegations

Mr. Judd of Illinois moved for a Committee of one Delegate from each State and territory represented to report officers for a permanent organization. The following is the Committee: . . . . The roll call of the states was read. As each Southern State and Territory represented was called, loud cheers were given. When the list was concluded, on a suggestion, the Delegates of the absent States were called, Alabama, Mississippi, and South Carolina being received with hisses.

Committees

On motion of Mr. BENTON, of New-Hampshire, a Committee on credentials was appointed.

Mr. BLANE of Pennsylvania moved for a Committee of one from each State and Territory to report order of business for the Convention. The following were appointed: . . . .

The rules of the House of Representatives were adopted for the government of the Convention.

HORACE GREELEY, delegate from Oregon, moved that the roll of States be called, and that the chairman of each delegation present the credentials thereof, and if there be any contest that the same be referred to the Committee on Credentials.

Mr. CARTER of Ohio moved to amend the proposition of the gentleman from Oregon or New-York, he did not know which, that the credentials be presented to the Committee. [As noted, Greeley, a prominent New Yorker, was attending at the invitation of the Oregon chairman as a delegate from that state, making him the butt of many jokes.]

HORACE GREELEY – I accept the amendment of the gentleman from Maryland or Rhode Island, I am not particular which. [Loud laughter.]

The motion was adopted.

It was announced that the Board of Trade having invited the delegates to an excursion on Lake Michigan at 5 o'clock p.m. [The Chicago Board of Trade exists today as part of the CME Group.]

Judge Goodrich of Minnesota, in moving the acceptance of the invitation, paid a compliment to the people of Chicago for the liberality and enterprise displayed in the erection and decoration of a fine hall for the meeting of the Convention.

An enthusiastic delegate here proposed three cheers for the ladies of Chicago.

The Convention compromised with one cheer....

A long discussion took place on a motion that when the Convention adjourn it be to five o'clock p.m. which eventually prevailed.

Mr. JOSHUA R. GIDDINGS,, of Ohio, was received with loud cheers. He moved to reconsider the vote accepting an invitation of the Board of Trade and called attention to the action of another Convention, which had worried the public mind with the length of their discussions. [The Democrats, at their convention in Charleston, South Carolina, a month earlier, had spent two weeks casting 57 ballots before having to adjourn, unable to pick a candidate.] *He hoped this Convention would finish all business by 3 o'clock to-morrow afternoon. [Loud applause.] The vote was reconsidered and Committee approved to confer with the Board of Trade and fix a future time for the excursion.*

The Convention then adjourned to 5 o'clock p.m.

Special dispatch to the <u>New York Tribune</u> –
between the morning and afternoon sessions:

CHICAGO, Wednesday, May 16 00 1 p.m.

The throng has largely increased to-day. There are 1,500 at the Tremont House alone, and not less than 10,000 strangers are here.

The opponents of Seward are confident that he will not be nominated. His friends for the first time show signs of wavering. Everything is confusion. Half the Convention are in doubt. Mr. Blair, senior, says Bates will be nominated, however large a vote is required.

The disorder and want of unity among the opponents of Seward begin to disappear, but they will probably be unable, and will not attempt, to agree upon one candidate, at least at present. Only two of the Pennsylvania delegation will go for Mr. Seward in any event.

Massachusetts having asked the States that protested against Seward whom they could carry, Pennsylvania names McLean, Lincoln, and Cameron; Illinois, Lincoln only.

REGULAR REPORT OF THE PROCEEDINGS.

-- AFTERNOON SESSION.

The Wigwam was again crowded to overflowing – a flock of people pouring in through every door as soon as it was opened, filling the Hall almost instantly with a densely-packed mass from the platform to the doors.

The galleries were also well filled with ladies, though not as compactly as at the morning session.

Mr. LOWRY of Pennsylvania reported that the Board of

Trade had prepared a large fleet for an excursion on the lake, and would wait till 6 o'clock for the Convention. He moved that the Convention attend the excursion at 6 o'clock. Lost, amid applause from the body of the hall.

Appointment of the Chairman

Mr. HORTON of Ohio, from the Committee on Permanent Organization, reported the name of George Ashmun of Massachusetts for permanent President. [Ashmun, a lawyer from Springfield, Massachusetts, had been Speaker of the Massachusetts legislature, a U.S. Congressman from 1845 through 1851, and an original founder of the Republican Party.]

The report was received with loud applause.

The Hon. Preston King of New-York and Carl Schurz of Wisconsin were appointed a Committee to conduct the President to the chair.

Mr. ASHMUN, on taking the chair, was greeted with immense applause the delegates rising and giving him six hearty cheers. When order was restored, he spoke as follows:

GENTLEMEN OF THE CONVENTION, REPUBLICANS AND AMERICANS: My first duty is to express to you my deep sense of this distinguished mark of your confidence; and in the spirit in which it is offered I accept. ... Gentlemen, it does not belong to me to make any extended address,.... but allow me to say I think we have a right here to-day, in the name of the American people, to impeach the Administration of our General Government of the highest crimes that can be committed against a constitutional Government, against a free people, and against humanity. [Prolonged cheers.] The catalogue of its crimes it is not for me to recite – it is written on every page of the history of the present Administration of the Government, and I care not how many paper protests the President may send in to the House of Representatives. [Laughter and applause.] . . . . I hail it as an augury of success, and if, during the proceedings of the Convention, you will unite to perpetuate that feeling and allow it to pervade all your proceedings, I declare to you it will be the surest and brightest omen of our success whoever may be the standard-bearer in the great contest that is pending. [Applause.] In that spirit gentlemen, let us now proceed to business – to the great work which the American people have given into our hands to do. [Loud cheers.]

Mr. MARSH, from the Committee on Permanent Organization, reported the following as Vice-Presidents and Secretaries: . . . . The names of Messrs. Marshall, Noyes, Stevens, Crawford, Davis, and Burlingame were received with loud cheers.

Mr. Judd of Illinois, on the part of C.G. Thomas, a working Republican of Chicago, presented to the chair a handsome gravel. He said it was not the wood, ivory, and silver alone which made it valuable. It was precious in consequence of association, being a piece of oak from the flag-ship of the gallant Lawrence. [Cheers.] [The

Lawrence was the original flagship of Commodore Oliver Perry when he fought the Battle of Lake Erie during the War of 1812.] *It was an emblem of the Republican party, strong and not noisy. The motto it bore was one which need not be urged upon Republicans, "Don't give up the ship." He hoped that at the end of this conflict the Republicans would be able to say with another great commander, "We have met the enemy, and they are ours." [Immense applause.]*

The PRESIDENT accepted the present on the part of the National Convention, in a few graceful remarks, declaring that the Republicans would observe the mottoes, and never would give up the ship. [Applause.]

Mr. TRACEY of California moved for a Committee of one from each State and Territory on Resolutions, and that the Illinois resolutions be referred to said Committee. Adopted without debate. The following Committee was appointed: . . . .

When the name of HORACE GREELEY of Oregon was announced, it was received with loud cheers and laughter. [Greeley would end up being the principal author of the Platform, adopted by the Convention the next day.]

Mr. ROLLINS of New-Hampshire moved that each delegate report the name of one person to constitute a member of the Republican National Committee for the ensuing four years. Carried.

Adjourned till 10 o'clock to-morrow.

Special dispatch to the _New York Tribune_.

CHICAGO, Wednesday, May 16 00

6:30 o'clock p.m. – The scene presented in the Hall during the sittings of the Convention is one of the finest and most impressive that can be imagined. The delegates and substitutes, a body of nearly one thousand, are arranged by States upon the platform. The reporters and leading editors occupy seats, to the number of eighty, in the center. Several hundred other editors are assigned seats in the galleries.

The vast galleries are otherwise crowded by a brilliant diversification of ladies and gentlemen, and the area in front of the platform, beneath the galleries, was crowded by men standing. Altogether 10,000 people were gathered to-day as participators or spectators, and the animation passing, as by electric shocks, through them, made them one in sympathy and action. The temptation of such an audience was too much for the delegates, and every opportunity to "orationize" was early sought and freely used. Its responses and interruptions by the audience was also a hindrance to the business of the Convention, but it lent great dignity and beauty to the spectacle. All seemed to feel that they were here not only as

Abraham Lincoln's Convention:

delegates and in sympathy, but in persons also.

Mr. Lincoln is rapidly assuming prominence as the candidate of the opposition to Mr. Seward, and if the latter's friends stick to him too long, the former may be nominated over their heads. Pennsylvania's naming Mr. Lincoln in preference to Mr. Bates, seems fatal to the latter. ... All New-England could be transferred to Mr. Lincoln more readily than to Mr. Bates. The North-Western States, refusing the latter, prefer Mr. Lincoln, next to Mr. Seward. Ohio, failing in her own candidates, would go to him, and Indiana is already divided between Messrs. Bates and Lincoln, with a majority for the latter. Iowa is also for Mr. Lincoln, and "honest old Abe" seems now the coming man. Mr. Banks or Mr.[John] Hickman [Congressman from Pennsylvania] *would probably be the Vice-President with him.*

11:25 P.M. – The latest horoscope to-night shows alarm and confusion both among the friends and opponents of Mr. Seward.

New-Jersey threatens to go over to Mr. Seward and leave Mr. Dayton.

Kentucky, which is bidding for the Vice-Presidency for Cassius M. Clay, divides its votes between Messrs. Seward and Chase.

Virginia is still pursued, and claimed for Mr. Seward.

The Texas delegation, which is made up mostly here, is all for Mr. Seward, and will be denounced as bogus to-morrow in the Convention....

A ballot is expected to be reached before night to-morrow....

Mr. Chase's friends talk of withdrawing him before a ballot is had. Less than half of the Ohio delegation are really for him, though they agree to give him their full vote on the first ballot. ... Ohio's order of preference is, Messrs. Chase, Wade, and Lincoln....

The Platform Committee is in labor to-night. There is a general disposition to be short and sharp, dealing in general propositions rather than specific policies. There will be an attempt to avoid indorsing the Wilmot Proviso specifically.

Mr. Ashman made a fine impression as presiding officer. He was not the choice of the Seward men...

1 a.m. – Mr. Weed was badly frightened this morning. He partially recovered to-night. New-Hampshire and Vermont staggered him. One of Mr. Seward's friends telegraphed him that the opposition was much stronger than was expected. A majority of the Convention is undoubtedly against Mr. Seward, but their difficulty is they have no candidate.

The Platform Committee is loaded down with propositions. They will report the Philadelphia Platform [the Platform from the party's first Convention in 1856], *revised and improved.*

GOV. SEWARD'S NOMINATION MORE PROBABLE,

by Horace Greeley

Special dispatch to *The New York Tribune*.

CHICAGO, Wednesday, May 16 – 10:40 p.m.

As to the President, I can only say that the advocates of Gov. Seward's nomination, who were much depressed last night, are now quite confident of his success. The changes on which their new hopes are based have been effected in the Virginia and New-Jersey delegations. I should say that the chances of his nomination are now about even. Mr. Lincoln now appears to have the next best look.

H.G. [Horace Greeley]

6. MAY 17: DAY TWO-
CREDENTIALS, RULES, PLATFORM

Dominating the second day of the Convention would be a fight over party rules, including (a) how many votes would be needed to select a presidential nominee and (b) how many seats would be given to small delegations from slave-holding states. Both sides viewed these as a test of strength for Seward's forces at the Convention.

From the _New York Tribune_, Friday morning, May 18, 1860.

THE CHICAGO CONVENTION

THE MAJORITY RULE ADOPTED.

THE PLATFORM

MR. SEWARD STILL IN THE ASCENDANT.

NO BALLOTING YET.

REGULAR REPORT OF THE PROCEEDINGS.

CHICAGO, Thursday, May 17, 1860.

The morning opened with much excitement. The streets were crowded, and there were several processions headed by bands of music. By invitation of the Michigan delegation, the New-York delegation and visitors gathered at the Adams House to march together to the "Wigwam."

The procession was the striking feature of the morning. They marched in sections of four, consisting of two from New-York and two from Michigan. The men numbering between 3,000 and 4,000 all wearing badges inscribed: "New-York Republican Association," "Michigan Republican Association," and with the name of Seward for President. A banner with Mr. Seward's likeness was carried at the head. Several bands of music were in the line. The procession stopped at different points, giving and receiving cheers.

The Convention was called to order at 10 o'clock.

10 o'clock, a.m. – Every part of the Wigwam is as densely crowded as yesterday.

Owing to the unprecedented number present, considerable time is consumed in obtaining order.

The Convention was opened by a prayer from the Rev. Mr. PATTEN of Chicago.

An invitation extended to the Delegates to take a trip over the Rock Island Railroad to Davenport, Iowa, by the President of that Company, was laid on the table.

A letter was then read asking the President if he could not send some effective speaker to entertain 20,000 Republicans and their wives [laughter] outside the building. The letter was greeted with loud cheers.

The Rules Fights

[Six slave states sent delegations to Chicago, but these states had few actual Republican voters and little or no party structure. As a result, questions arose over how to seat them. These delegations were seen as being stacked with Seward supporters. The fight focused on two issues, detailed below: (a) the 304-vote rule and (b) the seating of Maryland, Kentucky, and Virginia.]

R. M. CORWIN of Ohio, from the Committee on Rules of Order, reported a series for the Convention.

The first rule, giving a list of the States in order, was found to have omitted the State of New-York, which excited much laughter.

New-York protested against the omission.

Among the rules was the following:

"That four votes be cast by Delegates at Large and two for each Congressional District; that three hundred and four votes shall be considered a majority of the whole number of votes when all states in the Union are represented, and that the Convention on this ratio be required to nominate candidates." [This is the 304-vote rule, discussed below.]

Loud cries of "No!" "No!" with mingled cheers and hisses.

Mr. JAMES of New-York desired to say that only seventeen out of twenty-seven States were represented when the rule requiring 304 votes was adopted by one majority by the Committee. He presented as a minority report a substitute for said rule requiring a majority of all the votes cast to nominate. [Cheers and hisses.]

Mr. CARTER of Ohio said this was an important period of the proceedings. He called for the report of the Committee on Credentials, and moved that the report on the rules lie on the table for the present. Carried.

Mr. BENTON of New-Hampshire, from the Committee on Credentials, then reported no contested seats from twenty-four States. Pennsylvania had sent four from each Congressional District, and Iowa eight.

How many seats for Maryland, Kentucky, Virginia, and Texas?

[Theoretically, Republican Party rules gave each state a "full vote" equal to twice its number of votes in the Electoral College, that is, two seats for each Congressional district and four statewide seats at large. For these southern states, however, a "full vote" was seen as disproportionate power since they had few Republicans and little party organization. In some cases, it was unclear who actually sent these delegates, or whom they represented. Hence the effort to cut them back.]

Mr. DAVIS of Massachusetts moved to refer back the State of Texas to the Committee.

Mr. WILMOT of Pennsylvania moved to refer back, also, the

States of Maryland, Kentucky, and Virginia. This was a representative body, and men who represent no constituencies should not come here with a full vote. Such practices would demoralize and break up the party. In Maryland thirty persons had gathered at Baltimore and sent delegates here. There was no party organization there, and would be none until the Republicans had wrested the Government from the hands of its present possessors. These delegates represent no Republican constituency, and if the precedent is established, there will soon be delegates in the Republican Convention from every State of the Union. They had been sent there to demoralize and break up the party, and in favor of some Northern intrigue. One mischievous rule had been adopted when these States were admitted, and the other objectionable rule, requiring a majority of all the States in the Union to nominate, grew out of this. He denied the right of these men, respectable as they were, to pretend to represent Republican constituents. [Loud cheers].

Mr. EWING of Pennsylvania deprecated the sentiments of his colleague. [Loud applause, and cries of "That's the talk!"] These men from the Slave States were entitled to credit than many others, and we would not consent to disfranchise them. [Cheers, and cries of "No! No!"] He was astonished to hear the sentiments expressed by his colleague. These men are bold, earnest Republicans. They represent the Republicans of the Southern States; and if in numbers they are small, we hope to make them greater. [Loud cheers.]

Mr. PALMER of Maryland said that he stood before this free Convention as a Republican of the State of Maryland. [Cheers, and three cheers for Maryland.] He claimed to be as good a Republican as any of the People's Party of Pennsylvania. He had dared more and risked more than the gentlemen from Pennsylvania had ever raised or dared. He had avowed himself a Republican, while the People's party of Pennsylvania were still afraid to declare themselves thorough Republicans. [Immense applause.] He had been jeered by a mob in Baltimore, and on his return home had been burned in effigy, and hung by the neck by a mob led on by Federal officeholders. He claimed that if the party hoped to succeed, they must organize throughout the Union. He repelled the accusation that Maryland was the tool of any Northern State. They were unpurchased and unpurchasable, and they told Pennsylvania to put that in its pipe and smoke it. [Immense cheers.] He cared not if Maryland was turned out of this Convention. [Cries of "No," "No," "it never shall be."] They would still go home, and run an electoral ticket. [Cheers.] He felt from the applause so kindly bestowed that he had not appealed in vain to the fair and honorable sentiments of the people.

Three hearty cheers were given for Maryland.

Mr. BLAKEY of Kentucky was surprised on his entrance to the Convention to find a proposition to banish Kentucky from the Convention. He should not have been more surprised had a proposition been made to banish Washington from beyond the limits *of the union; that the sacred dust of Ashland should be banished beyond the borders of that State; that Cassius M. Clay should be sent into exile. [Cheers.]* [Kentuckian Cassius M. Clay, a cousin of Whig Founder Henry Clay and a rare abolitionist in the slave-holding south, is best known today as the namesake for the heavy weight boxing champion who later changed his name to Mohammad Ali.] *Who would dare to banish the free sons of Kentucky, or of Maryland, or of Texas, or the District of Columbia, from this Convention? He was a member of the Republican Convention in 1856 – a seat his children should live to be proud of – and then and there on the part of Kentucky he had risen, and with the memory of the Wilmot Proviso before him, had cast the vote of Kentucky for the Vice-Presidency for David Wilmot of Pennsylvania. [Loud applause and cheers.] Could he ever be forgiven for that act? [Renewed laughter and applause.]*

Mr. PHILLIPS of Kansas said he stood here as the representative from the Territory which would have been a State to day but for its fidelity to Republicanism. He did not believe that any man would desire to banish Kansas from the Convention. [Cheers, and cries for Wilmot.]

Mr. WILMOT took the platform. He regretted he had been misunderstood. He made no proposition to exclude the gentlemen from the Convention. He had simply moved to refer back certain States to the Committee to decide what vote the several States shall be entitled to. In order to enforce the argument, he asked why 30 persons in Baltimore and representing on constituency throughout the State should be entitled to vote here for the State.

Mr. PALMER of Maryland explained that the meeting in Baltimore, although small, was held under the regular call of the Republican organizations; nearly every Congressional district in the State was represented.

Mr. WILMOT said the explanation made would enforce the propriety of his motion. He only desired that the Committee should investigate whether in these States there is a regular Republican organization to entitle them to voices here.... If the Committee reported that the States have a regular organization and took regular action, and were entitled to votes, he should willingly accept the reports. It was rumored that the delegates from Texas were not residents there. It might be said that the delegates from Oregon were not residents there; but there was a regular and powerful Republican organization there, and the powers had been delegated to non-residents. If Texas had regularly delegated these gentlemen as representatives, all was well; but, if they only came here to control the nominations, it was a dangerous and fatal precedent. .... He made no issue as to who dared suffer most in the Republican cause, but if this is to be the test, Kansas should control this Convention, for she had poured out her blood in the Republican cause. ...

Loud cries of "Question," "Question."....

Gov. CLEVELAND said he regarded this whole movement as pernicious. ... The Republicans desired to make no war on the

Slave States.   That was an invention of the enemy, and he called on the Convention to do no act that could look like sectionalism.

Mr. OYLER of Indiana called attention to the call for the National Convention, which he read..... The call had invited all who desired to overthrow the corrupt Democracy in the States to act with the Convention.   If not, they were the most arrant knaves and hypocrites.   They could not now deny the right of representation to the Slave States.   [Loud cheers.]   ....

Mr. BECKLAND of Michigan moved to amend by referring back the papers of Oregon to the Committee also....

Mr. HACKLEMAN of Indiana did not object to the admission of any State but Texas.   He did desire that the question should be investigated, and that the delegates from Texas should show who sent them there.

Mr. ------------- of Texas said he did not believe the Republicans would stifle the voice of Texas because she was an infant child.   She was at least growing. ... He regretted that the motion [to eject Texas] *should come from a gentleman from Pennsylvania – A State that was afraid even now to declare herself as a pure Republican organization, and did not care to stand upon pure Republican principles alone.   [Cheers and hisses from Pennsylvania.]   Such action was contemptible and dastardly.* [Pennsylvania Republicans still referred to themselves as The People's Party, rather than as Republicans.]

Mr. LOWREY of Pennsylvania moved to re-commit the

entire report, and called for a vote by States. He regarded the report as an evasion of duty, for nothing respecting the titles of delegates to seats was mentioned.

Mr. BENTON of New-Hampshire said the sub-Committee had fully investigated the titles of delegates to seats, and were satisfied that all were regular.

The President decided that under the rules the votes of delegates could not be called, but for convenience the States were called.

The motion to recommit was carried – Yeas 275½, Nays 172½ . The following is the vote:

Maine, Ayes, 3; Nays, 13; New-Hampshire, Ayes, 1; Nays, 9; Vermont, Ayes, 9; Nays,1; Massachusetts, Ayes, 13; Nays, 9; Rhode-Island, Ayes, 8; Connecticut, Ayes, 10; Nays, 2; New-York; Ayes, 1; Nays, 69; New-Jersey, Ayes, 14; Pennsylvania, Ayes, 53½; Nays, 1½ ; Delaware, Ayes, 1; Nays, 5; Maryland, Ayes, 4; Nays, 6; Virginia, Ayes, 30; Ohio, Ayes, 45; Kentucky, Ayes, 24; Indiana, Ayes, 26; Michigan, Nays, 12; Illinois, Ayes, 22; Wisconsin, Nays, 10; Minnesota, Nays, 8; Iowa, Ayes, 8; Missouri, Ayes, 4; Nuys, 14; California, Ayes, 4; Nays, 3; Oregon, Nays, 5.

This vote created great interest and excitement. It was not, however, regarded as a test vote, as the Southern States voted Aye because of the delicacy of their position. [The effect of this vote was to reject "full" voting rights for these slave states and to require the Credentials Committee to develop a new formula.

Note (a) the lop-sided negative vote from New York representing Seward backers, (b) the absence of any votes from Alabama, Arkansas, Florida, Georgia, Louisiana, Mississippi, Tennessee, or the Carolinas, the southern states boycotting the convention, and (c) the split vote from Maryland.]

Special Dispatch to the *New York Tribune* —

between the sessions.

CHICAGO, Thursday, May 17, 1860.

The Committee on Credentials failing to make an exact report as to Texas, the Territories, and the other disputed delegations, the morning session of the Convention was wholly occupied in discussing those questions. The report was finally recommitted. The Texas vote was not a test, though the leading Seward States voted No, and were defeated by one hundred votes.

The Business Committee proposes a rule that a majority of the whole Electoral College, or 304 delegates, be required to nominate. This will be resisted by the Seward men, and probably will be made a test; its adoption defeats him surely. No prospects of a ballot for President to-day.

REGULAR REPORT OF THE PROCEEDINGS - continued.

The Convention reassembled with the largest number of spectators yet present, every inch of room being filled in every part of the building.

The platform was further embellished with a large number of framed portraits of eminent patriots and statesmen, and the handsome banners of the Young Men's Republican Union of New-York and the Ward Republican Clubs of Chicago.

Under a portrait of Broderick, draped in mourning, appeared the inscription, "They have killed me because I was opposed to the extension of Slavery, and to a corrupt Administration." [As noted, David C. Broderick, a United States Senator from California, had been killed in September 1859 in a duel with the leader of a pro-slavery Democratic group.]

At 3 o'clock the Convention was called to order.

The PRESIDENT announced that there were twice the number of honest hearts outside, who had, through a Committee, requested Gov. Randall of Wisconsin to address them on the political questions of the day. [Loud applause.]

Back to the Credentials Fight

Mr. BENTON of New-Hampshire, from the Committee on Credentials, again reported, giving the State of Virginia 23 votes, Kentucky, 23; Oregon, 5; Maryland, 11, and Texas, 6. In regard to the organization in Texas, the Committee reported that the delegates were elected at a meeting, rallied by notice in all the papers favorable to Republican principles, and were entitled to seats. [This compromise reduced the voting power of Virginia and Kentucky and allowed participation by Texas.]

The report was adopted amid applause.

The vote in these States is cut down below the full double electoral vote.

How big a majority to choose a nominee?

The report of the Committee on Business and Rules was then taken up.

The second rule, giving the at-large delegates four votes, and each Congressional representation two votes, except as modified by the Committee was amended by providing that no more votes shall be cast than there are delegates present, and adopted.

On the fourth rule being read, which provides that 304 votes, being a majority of the whole double electoral vote, shall be necessary to nominate candidates, the minority report to nominate by a majority of votes cast was moved as an amendment. [This fourth rule – the requirement for a 304 majority -- was the key preliminary contest between Seward and his opponents. Here's the math: Theoretically, the Republican Convention rules gave each state two Convention votes for each vote it had in the Election College – two for each Senator and Congressman – or a maximum of 606 Convention votes total, making a majority of 304. However, since nine slave states (Alabama, Arkansas, Florida, Georgia, Louisiana, Mississippi, Tennessee, or the Carolinas) were boycotting the convention and six others (Delaware, Maryland, Virginia, Kentucky, Missouri, and Texas) sent smaller delegations, this theoretical majority would require almost two-thirds of the actual sitting delegates and give disproportionate power to the small Southern delegations. Opponents of the rule preferred to let a simple majority of sitting delegates pick the nominee. The Democratic Party since 1844 had applied a two-thirds rule intended to give Southern slave-holding states a veto in choosing presidential nominees.]

Mr. KELLEY of Pennsylvania said this subject was one of the most important that could arise. It had been carefully considered by the Committee. It had been felt that, under the rule, this was a National Convention of the Republican Party, and as such it was deemed that the nominees should receive a majority of the vote of the electoral college, comprising not only the people of the Northern or border Slave States, but the people of the United States. If any State is absent, whether by design or accident, the Convention does not cast her vote for her, but save she shall have a voice in the selection of candidates;... These were the main considerations that influenced the Committee, but other considerations of much weight confirmed their action. The Convention knew there were some gentlemen here from States, honored wherever courage is honored, but where there are but few Republicans. ... When the Committee considered that these delegates would be admitted with a full electoral vote, they feared that unless this rule was adopted, the nominee of the party might be such as would not have a majority of the votes represented actually having Republican votes to offer to the party. There were the motives which influenced the Committee's action.

Judge JAMES of New-York, on the part of the minority, said a rule had already been adopted by the Convention which gives 446 votes as a full vote of the Convention. The minority has therefore substantially a two-third vote – 304 being only seven votes short of two-thirds. This was the rule of Democratic Conventions, and had been suggested in order to carry out the Democratic policy of allowing the minority to rule the majority. [Great applause.] If the majority report, giving negative votes to absent Southern States, should be adopted, the same policy would be initiated here, and to this he was opposed. [Loud applause.]

W.B. MANN of Pennsylvania said he came from a State where the majority ruled. He knew no reason why it should be otherwise here. If the majority rule should prevail, it would seem like a secret blow at a candidate who had done no wrong. [Loud and prolonged applause.]

Loud cries of "Question – question," and a vote by States was demanded.

When Pennsylvania was called, they asked for time.

Mr. GOODRICS of Minnesota asked that the representatives of the People's party of Pennsylvania be excused from voting.

Cries of "Order – order;" and hisses.

Mr. REEDER of Pennsylvania said that the delegates from Pennsylvania had found it necessary to retire to consult. He understood some persons to say that the People's party of the State had no right to vote. He desired to know the name of that gentleman. [Cheers, and cries of "order."]

Mr. GOODRICH said he had not questioned the right of the People's party to vote, but the name of the State having been called for the fourth time, and the delegates unable to vote on their own proposition, he asked that they be excused from voting out of feelings of humanity.

The vote was announced, and the minority rule as then reported by Judge James, requiring a majority of the votes cast only to nominate, was adopted, 331 Yeas; 130 nays. [Loud and prolonged applause.]

The rules as amended were then adopted.

Special Dispatch to the <u>New York Tribune</u>.

CHICAGO, Thursday, May 17, 1860.

9 p.m. – The afternoon session cleared the deck for the nomination, which is the first and only business to-morrow. The

Slave States were pared down to their actual number of delegates present Kansas and Nebraska were admitted, and the District of Columbia allowed two votes. The whole number of votes now in the Convention, is now 466.

The opponents of Seward shrank from making a test of the proposition making 304 or a majority of the Electoral Colleges a requisite of the nomination. Some thought it unnecessary as a measure to defeat Seward, but the characterization of it [the 304-vote rule] *as borrowed from a Democratic Convention where it was adopted in the guise of the two-third rule by the Southern States to preserve their waning numerical power, turned more against it and it was defeated by two to one. Its introduction greatly frightened the Seward men, and they feel themselves relieved by its failure.*

REGULAR REPORT OF THE PROCEEDINGS - continued.

Judge Jessup from the Committee on resolutions reported the following:

THE PLATFORM   [The full text of the Platform was read at this point. See Appendix.]

When the resolutions were read, several elicited warm applause.

The resolution in favor of a Projective Tariff was received with unbounded enthusiasm by Pennsylvania, and a large crowd of outsiders – the whole delegation and spectators rising, and giving round after round of deafening cheers.

Mr. CARTER of Ohio said he was confident that all approved of the resolutions, and therefore moved the previous question.

Mr. GIDDINGS of Ohio asked his colleagues to withdraw the call for the previous question, in order to enable him to offer an amendment to the platform.

Mr. CARTER refused to withdraw.

Mr. GIDDINGS – Does my colleague desire to cut off amendments?

Mr. CARTER – You, and all others. I desire to get a vote on the resolutions.

After some skirmishing, the Convention refused to order the previous question by 155 to 301.

Giddings amendment

Mr. GIDDINGS of Ohio moved to add to the first resolution the following:

"That we solemnly re-assert with self-evident truths, that all men are endowed by the Creator with certain inalienable rights, among which are those of life, liberty, and the pursuit of happiness; that governments are intended among men to secure the enjoyment of these rights." [The Platform already cited this language from the Declaration of Independence, but the Giddings amendment was seen as going farther and demanding social

equality for African Americans, including the right to vote. Hence the controversy. Giddings, a 74-year Congressman from Ohio, was a long-time anti-slavery advocate who had been active in the Underground Railroad and had condemned the annexation of Texas and the Mexican War.]

Mr. CARTER of Ohio – I desire to move an amendment.

Mr. GIDDINGS – I have the floor, and hope my colleague will ask no favor of me.

Mr. CARTER – O no, I will not.

Mr. GIDDINGS urged the adoption of his amendment. The great principle it embodied had been the foundation of Freedom for two hundred years. The fathers of the Republic had embodied it in the Declaration of Independence, and he urged upon the Republican party not to recede from the position they had occupied at the first formation of the party, when they had based the fabric of Freedom on these very words. He urged . . . . .the amendment at some length.

Mr. CARTER said it was all gas and had been expended by his colleague on the amendment. It was unnecessary as the substance of the words was embodied in the second resolution which he read.

ELI THAYER of Oregon, said that the amendment of the gentleman from Ohio certainly embodied great truths, but many great truths had been left out of the declaration of independence. He for one believed in the Ten Commandments, but he did not desire to see them embodied in the platform. [Applause].

The motion and amendment were then lost by a large vote.

...

Immigration

CARL SCHURZ, in relation to the naturalization laws, said that the German Republicans of the North-west had in 1856 given the Republicans 300,000 votes. They asked this resolution in order to know whether they can with safety and self-respect give it 300,000 again. At Philadelphia they asked only one general declaration against any interference with the rights of naturalized citizens, but since it had been found that State Legislatures passed laws assailing the rights of naturalized citizens, it was now asked that the Republican party should denounce such legislation. On one side was right, on the other was prejudice. Could the party gain more from prejudice than from right? [Great applause.] The German Republicans were disinterested friends of the principles of the party. They came to its ranks, not for office or for profit, but for the hope of liberty, and from a sense of the correctness of its principles.

[In addition to fairness for immigrants, Schurz's proposal was also seen as a strike against "Know Nothings," the powerful anti-immigrant group present in many states.]

Judge HASSAUREK of Cincinnati made an elegant address expressing his devotion to Republican principle and the true Americanism. He had learned his love of liberty from the study of the life of Washington. His heart was imbued with American principles before he took the oath of allegiance to his adopted Government. His speech was ardent and eloquent, and was loudly applauded throughout.

Judge JESSUP desired to amend a verbal mistake in the name of the party. It was printed in the resolution National Republican party. He wished to strike out the word national, and that was not the name by which the party was properly known. The correction was made.

Re-raising the Giddings Amendment

G.W. CURTIS of New-York moved to amend the second resolution by adding thereto the prelude to the Declaration of Independence. [Curtis, in 1860 still a young writer for Greeley's Tribune and Putnam's Magazine, would in 1863 become political editor of Harper's Weekly and use this platform to become one of the pre-eminent voices for political reform in Gilded Age America.]

ELI THAYER raised a point of order that the amendment had already been voted down.

The PRESIDENT ruled the point of order well taken.

FRANCIS P. BLAIR said that if necessary, he would appeal from the chair. The former amendment was made to the first resolution, while the proposition was to amend the second resolution.

The PRESIDENT – If such is the case, the amendment is in

order.

Mr. CURTIS said that this was the second National Convention of the Republican party, and he asked whether the party was not prepared to vote down the words of the Declaration of Independence. He cautioned them to beware before here, in the broad prairies of the West, they receded from the position they had occupied at Philadelphia, and refused to repeat the words of the fathers of the Revolution as used in the Declaration of American Independence. [Loud applause.]

Mr. OYLER of Indiana, said that he believed in the Declaration of Independence, but was it necessary to put them in the platform? [Loud shouts of "Yes," "yes"]. He was told it was – then he would say that it was already in. [Cries of "Put in twice."]. He thought it would be as proper to put in the Bible from the first chapter to the last.

Gen. NYE now took the floor, and was proceeding to speak, when several delegates from Pennsylvania said, "put it in and say no more about it."

Gen. NYE – That, gentlemen, is all I want, and I am glad that the fear of a speech from me has induced gentlemen to give way. [Laughter and applause.] The amendment was then adopted.

The resolution, as amended, was passed unanimously. [As a result, both the Giddings language and the Carl Schurz pro-immigrant amendment were adopted.]

A scene of the wildest excitement followed, the immense

multitude rising, and giving round after round of applause; 10,000 voices swelled into a roar so deafening that for several minutes every attempt to restore order was hopelessly vain. The multitude outside took up and reechoed the cheers, making the scene of enthusiasm and excitement unparalleled in any similar gathering.

Amid the confusion, it was motioned to adjourn till 10 o'clock to-morrow. Lost.

Mr. GOODRICH of Minnesota moved to ballot for a candidate for President.

Much confusion and cries of "Ballot" ensued, amid which the President put the affirmative on the motion to adjourn, and declared the Convention adjourned till 10 to-morrow.

Special Dispatch to the <u>New York Tribune</u>.

CHICAGO, Thursday, May 17, 1860.

9 p.m. –The platform gives great satisfaction, and the demonstrations of applause on its adoption both by the Convention and among the audience were most enthusiastic, and lasted some moments. It seemed well nigh impossible to stop the hurrahs. When the tariff resolution was read there was great rejoicing, more than over any other one resolution.

Mr. Giddings moved to recite the Declaration of Independence, in terms as amendment to the original report, but the Anti-Negro Suffrage State opposed it, and it was lost. Mr. Giddings then retired, vexed and sad. Afterward. Mr. Geo. W. Curtis proposed it again, and made a brief and telling speech which carried the Convention, and the amendment was adopted without a count, by three to one.

There were no Nays to the platform, and consequently no vote by States.

There was an attempt by Mr. Wilmot to modify the Anti-Know-Nothing [or pro-immigrant] *resolution, but he early abandoned it. Carl Schurz's speech for this resolution was very fine, and won the Convention to him and to it.*

The friends of Mr. Seward say the platform just fits him. His opponents say it is so radical that it needs a Conservative candidate to harmonize the elements, and get the votes of the doubtful States.

11:45 p.m. – The feeling that Mr. Seward is to be nominated has been increasing all day, and is still dominant. Strenuous efforts are making to-night on both sides, and the opposition reports some gains; but so do the Seward men.

They claim that Vermont has returned, that New-Hampshire is divided, and that there is a general yielding all around in their behalf. It is impossible to count up the Seward vote to a majority, but unless the opposition can demonstrate the possibility of carrying up a vote for some one as high as his, and their determination to hold firm to the last, he will be nominated after a few ballots to-morrow....

Illinois, Indiana, and Pennsylvania, say that with this

platform, and Mr. Seward, they are beaten beyond all hope in the latter States by 20,000 to 50,000. There will be no election by the people with Mr. Seward, and the choice of John Bell by the House is a very common judgment. [The concern here was that if Seward and Democrat Stephen A. Douglas both failed to win an outright majority in the Electoral College -- not unlikely with four candidates in the race -- the choice of President would be made by the House of Representatives, with each state having one vote. And in this arena, John Bell, candidate of the newly-formed Constitutional Union Party, would have an advantage because he had served as Speaker of the House during the 1830s.]

The friends of Mr. Lincoln want 100 votes for him on the first ballot, against 170 for Mr. Seward.

Mr. Raymond of The N. Y. Times is here working for Mr. Seward, and The Times will support him if nominated. John Wentworth's influence is also for Mr. Seward, and he says he can carry Illinois. [John Wentworth, the Republican mayor of Chicago, was a rival of Lincoln's in state politics and supported Seward for the nomination.]

Midnight. – Though there is an increased disposition to gather about Mr. Lincoln, no effective combination of opposition is yet formed. Ohio is uncertain, Pennsylvania gives no positive assurances, and when New-Jersey breaks but half goes to Mr.

Seward. Part of the Missouri delegations prefer Mr. Seward to Mr. Lincoln.

They want a conservative with whom to make a winning fight, or a straight-out radical for contest of pure principle.

New-England is anxious and doubtful. She is puzzled. They hesitate both to desert Mr. Seward and force him on the doubtful States. They are likely to be much eaten up. The Massachusetts delegation has been in a labored conference, and show an increased disposition to leave Mr. Seward, and go for Mr. Lincoln.

There is no telling what the morrow will bring forth. Probably Mr. Seward – but by no means is that certain to-night. Leading Opposition men are down-hearted, and say that with a majority and the convictions of the Convention against Mr. Seward, he is still likely to be nominated. The Seward men are full of hope and joy, but cannot give their figures. As for the Platform, its Anti-Know-Nothing planks are much denounced as an undue pandering to German fanaticism.

GOV. SEWARD WILL BE NOMINATED, by Horace Greeley. Special to the _New York Tribune._

CHICAGO, Thursday, May 17 – 11:40 p.m.

My conclusion, from all that I can gather, to-night, is that the opposition to Gov. Seward cannot concentrate on any candidate, and that he will be nominated.

_H.G._ [Horace Greeley]

Greeley would later explain this note in a signed editorial on May 22, a few days after the convention: _At the last moment – that is, on the night before the nomination – the selection of Gov. Seward seemed rendered inevitable by the obstinacy where-with the several rival candidates were adhered to by their respective friends. It was on the apparent impossibility of bringing even Ohio to unite on any candidate from without her own borders – (or from within either, for that matter) – that I telegraphed that Gov. Seward's nomination seemed inevitable. And, even when the Convention assembled on Friday morning, I could not see how a concentration of the anti-Seward force was to be effected, while the friends of Gov. S. – not by way of bravado, but in perfect good faith – inquired of the other side as to their preference for Vice-President, regarding their own success for the first place as a matter of course._

....

From *The New-York Times*,
   Written Friday morning, May 18 – by Joe Howard Jr.

[As of late Thursday night,] *the friends of Seward were devoted to him and his interests, and would stick with him so long as there was the faintest hope of success. The leaders were very sanguine of victory. THURLOW WEED said he "was sure of success." Mr. EVARTS said their "victory was certain, and would be rapid."*

A meeting of the opponents of Seward was held, at which efforts were made to harmonize the conflicting elements. The friends of LINCOLN, CAMERON, and BATES were there, but after a protracted session, nothing was accomplished, they adjourned.

View from inside the Lincoln camp:

Telegram to Abraham Lincoln from David Davis

May 17, 1860. Chicago, Illinois.
Lincoln papers. Library of Congress.

To Hon A Lincoln   Am very hopeful. Don't be Excited. Nearly dead with fatigue. Telegraph or write here very little.   David Davis

Lincoln's final instructions:

Note to David Davis from Abraham Lincoln, May 17, 1860.
Collected works of Abraham, Lincoln, Vol. IV.

Written in pencil on the margin of a page from the _Missouri Democrat,_ hand carried to Chicago, and delivered directly to Davis: "... *Make no contracts that will bind me.*"

Davis, on receiving it, reportedly said: *"Lincoln ain't here, and don't know what we have to meet. So we will go ahead as if we hadn't heard from him and he must ratify it."*

7.   MAY 18: DAY THREE- FOR PRESIDENT

From the *New York Tribune*, May 18, 1860.

THE LATEST NEWS.
Received By
MAGNETIC TELEGRAPH.

THE CHICAGO CONVENTION.

Naming of Candidates.

INTENSE ENTHUSIASM.

The Struggle between Seward and Lincoln.

LINCOLN NOMINATED.

ONLY THREE BALLOTINGS HAD.

THE VICE-PRESIDENCY.

Hon. Hannibal Hamlin Nominated.

HOW THE NOMINATIONS ARE RECEIVED.

Salutes, Bonfires and Pyrotechny.

GREAT JOY AND ENTHUSIASM.

REGULAR REPORT OF THE PROCEEDINGS.

Chicago, Friday, May 18, 1860.

The Wigwam was closely packed for a full hour before the Convention assembled this morning. The interest in the proceedings appears on the increase as the time for balloting approaches. A crowd numbered by thousands has been outside the building since 9 o'clock, anxiously awaiting intelligence from the inside. Arrangements have been made for passing the result of the ballots up from the platform to the roof of the building, and through the skylight, men being stationed above to convey speedily the intelligence to the multitude in the streets.

A large procession was formed by the various delegations to march to the hall, preceded by bands of music, New-York being by far the most numerous.

As the delegates entered on the platform the several distinguished men were greeted with rounds of applause by the audience.

The opening prayer was delivered by the Rev. Mr. Treen of the Tabernacle, Baptist Church.

Three or four meetings were held at a distance outside and during the silence of the prayer in the Convention, the roars and shouts of these meetings could be distinctly heard in the Wigwam.

The PRESIDENT, on opening the proceedings, begged the audience to refrain as much as possible from applause, and to preserve, as far as consistent, the decorum and dignity of the meeting.

The PRESIDENT announced an invitation for an excursion over the Chicago and Galena Railroad; also a communication from the workingmen of Brooklyn, Williamsburg, and Greenpoint, New-York, in favor of bestowing the Government lands on actual settlers, and for arresting the further sale of the public lands.

Both communications were ordered to be entered on the record.

The PRESIDENT announced the motion pending to be to take a ballot for a candidate for President of the United States.

Another quarrel over Maryland

Mr. Blair of Maryland announced that, in consequence of the adoption by the Convention of the rule restricting the vote of Maryland to the number of delegates present, the delegation had last evening filled up its number, and asked leave to present the credentials of five new delegates to fill the number from that State.

Mr. Sargeant of Chicago inquired whether the five additional votes now added would increase the vote to sixteen, or leave it at eleven, which was the number of votes assigned to that State by the report of the Committee on Credentials. If it desired to increase the vote above eleven, he was opposed to it.

W.T. Cole of Maryland said that his State had been entitled to eleven votes only, because the necessary number of delegates for the sixteen votes were not present. The delegation had power, by the action of the State Convention, to fill vacancies. They had now done so, under that authority, and claimed the right to and a full vote.

The PRESIDENT said he understood the rule adopted in the report of the Committee on Credentials to have restricted Maryland to eleven votes. The additional delegates would not entitle them to a greater vote.

Mr. Blair of Maryland desired to correct the error of the Chair. As he understood, the number was only limited because the delegates were not present. The delegation had a right to fill vacancies, and had done so in consequence of the rule adopted yesterday by the Convention.

Mr. Armour of Maryland protested against the reception of the credentials of new delegates. Eleven representatives only were present from his State. The delegation had met without his knowledge and without the knowledge of at least more than one delegate, and filled up their numbers with men who lived God only knows where. A resident of the State had been refused admission to the delegation, and what object his colleagues had in filling the delegation with non-residents he did not know. He hoped the motion to admit these delegates would be voted down.

The motion to admit the extra delegates was lost amid applause.

Nominations for President

The Convention then voted to proceed to ballot for a candidate for President of the United States.

Wm. M. Evarts of New-York did not rise for the purpose of making a speech, but only to ask if at this time it is in order to put candidates in nomination.

The PRESIDENT – The Chair considers it in order to name candidates without debate.

A delegate from Pennsylvania drew attention to the fact that delegates' seats were occupied by outsiders.

A Voice – The same here in Ohio.

The PRESIDENT – This affords an opportunity to the Chair to read a communication just received from the doorkeepers. The communication stated that delegates, as soon as they got into the hall, passed their tickets out to friends. The officers therefore found it impossible to prevent the admission of outsiders, but the fault rested with the delegates. [Early that morning, David Davis reportedly had packed the Wigwam with Lincoln supporters by printing thousands of tickets, handing them out to friends, and instructing them to come early and crowd out the Seward men who were busy that morning marching through Chicago with their brass band.]

The PRESIDENT suggested that the only method to pursue would be for each delegate to claim his own seat with vigor.

After some delay, occasioned by the clearing of the platform and distributing ballots, the Convention proceeded to ballot.

Wm. M. Evarts rose and said – I beg leave to offer the name of Wm. M. Seward as a candidate before this Convention for the nomination of President of the United States. [Evarts, in 1860 still a rising New York lawyer and former district attorney, would later become Secretary of State under President Rutherford Hayes, a United States Senator from New York, and chief counsel to President Andrew Johnson during his 1868 impeachment trial.]

This nomination was received with loud and long continued applause.

Mr. Judd of Illinois rose and said: Mr. President, I beg leave to offer as a candidate before this Convention for President of the United States the name of Abraham Lincoln of Illinois.

The crowded audience greeted this nomination with perfectly deafening applause, the shouts swelling into a perfect roar, and being continued for several minutes the wildest excitement and enthusiasm prevailing. At the close of the applause some hisses were heard, but the pressure for Lincoln was tremendous.

From Joe Howard Jr. of *The New-York Times*:

Mr. Judd, of Chicago, begged leave to suggest the name of Abram Lincoln, of Illinois.

If Mr. Seward's name drew forth thunders of applause, what can be said of the enthusiastic reception of this name Lincoln? I have never seen anything which compares with it. The greetings which Jenny Lind or Grisi or La Geange [famous actresses of the time] *at Castle Garden or the Academy of Music did not begin to equal that which I now record. Ten thousand people were in the Wigwam, and the crowd without could not be numbered. The vast throng rose simultaneously, hats and handkerchiefs were waved, cheers and hearty hurrahs were given, and the air seemed full of some magnetic influence, which moved all alike to exhibit to the full extent of their powers of lung and length of wind. The President rapped and ordered silence, but in vain. The audience, like a wild colt with bit between his teeth, rose above all cry of order, and again and again the irrepressible applause broke forth and resounded far and wide. The crowd outside took it up, and cheer after cheer from them indorsed the sentiments of their brethren within.*

After this scene was concluded, the names of other gentlemen were mentioned, and received with some applause, but all was cold when compared with that which greeted the names of those above.

REGULAR REPORT OF THE PROCEEDINGS – continued.

Mr. Dudley of New-Jersey presented the name of Wm. L. Dayton. [Light applause.]

Gov. Reeder of Pennsylvania. [Andrew H. Reeder, a

Pennsylvanian, actually served as territorial governor of Kansas prior to 1860, not as governor of Pennsylvania.] *The State of Pennsylvania desired to present as her candidate the name of Simon Cameron. [Applause.]*

Mr. Carter of Ohio put forward the name of Salmon P. Chase of Ohio. [Loud Applause.]

Mr. Smith of Maryland – I am instructed by the State of Indiana to second the nomination of Abraham Lincoln. [Another outburst of enthusiastic applause from the body of the Hall, mingled with some hisses.]

Francis P. Blair of Missouri nominated Edward Bates of Missouri. [Applause.]

Mr. Blair of Michigan said, on the part of Michigan I desire to say that the Republicans of that State second the nomination of Wm. H. Seward for the Presidency.

Tremendous applause followed, thousands of those present railing and waving their hats and handkerchiefs, and swelling the applause to a thundering roar through several minutes.

This was followed by some hisses and loud applause for Lincoln, when the friends of Seward again rallied, determined not to be put down in applause by the friends of Lincoln. At this second trial of lungs, however, it was evident that the crowd was more divided than at first appeared, and the Lincoln men apparently had the majority.

Tom Corwin of Ohio nominated John McLean of Ohio for the

Presidency. [Loud applause.]

Carl Schulz of Wisconsin, on the part of his State, here seconded the nomination of Wm. H. Seward.

Upon this, another scene of the greatest enthusiasm and simultaneous excitement ensued.

Mr. North of Minnesota also seconded, on the part of Minnesota, the Nomination of Mr. Seward. [Tremendous applause.]

Mr. Wilson of Kansas – The delegates and people of Kansas seconded the nomination. [Renewed cheers.]

Mr. Delano of Ohio, on the part of a large number of people of Ohio – I desire to second the nomination of the man who can split rails and maul Democrats. Abraham Lincoln. [Rounds of applause by Lincoln men.]

A delegate from Iowa also seconded the nomination of Mr. Lincoln, on the part of that State, amidst renewed applause and excitement.

A Voice – Abe Lincoln has it by the sound now. Let us ballot.

Cheers and hisses.

Judge Lugar of Illinois – Mr. President, in order or out of order, I propose this Convention and audience give three cheers for the man who is evidently their nominee.

The First Ballot

[Ballots, then as now, were announced by state as each state's name was called. The *Tribune* grouped the tallies by candidate for ease in transmitting them by telegraph.]

The first ballot results are as follows

For Mr. Seward.

Maine 10		Wisconsin 10	
New-Hampshire 1		Iowa 2	
Massachusetts 21		California 8	
New-York 70		Minnesota 8	
Pennsylvania 11/2		Kansas 6	
Maryland 3		Nebraska 2	
Virginia 8		District of Columbia 2	
Kentucky 5		Texas 4	
Michigan 12		Total 173 1/2	

For Mr. Lincoln.

Maine 6		Ohio 8	
New-Hampshire 7		Indiana 26	
Massachusetts 4		Illinois 22	
Connecticut 2		Iowa 2	
Pennsylvania 4		Nebraska 1	
Virginia 14			
Kentucky 6		Total 102	

For Mr. Bates.

Rhode Island 1		Texas 2	
Connecticut 7		Iowa 1	
Maryland 8		Oregon 5	
Delaware 6			
Missouri 18		Total 48	

For Mr. Cameron – Pennsylvania,47 1/2; Virginia, 1; Iowa, 1; Nebraska, 1 – Total 50 ½.

For Mr. McLean – Rhode Island, 5; Pennsylvania, 1; Kentucky, 1; Ohio, 4; total, 1 – Total 12.

For Mr. Chase – New-Hampshire, 1; Rhode Island, 1; Connecticut, 2; Kentucky 8; Iowa, 1; Ohio, 34; Nebraska, 2 – Total, 49.

For Mr. Wade – Connecticut, 1; Kentucky, 2; Total, 3.

For Mr. Dayton – New-Jersey, 14.

For Mr. Read – Rhode Island, 1.

For Mr. Fremont – New-Hampshire, 1.

For Mr. Collamer – Vermont, 10.

For Mr. Sumner – Kentucky, 1.

Whole number of votes, 465.
Necessary to a choice, 233.

From Joe Howard Jr. of <u>The New-York Times</u>:

The balloting, as telegraphed, was then commenced. At the close of the first ballot, it was evident that something was in the wind not known to outsiders generally. Quietly I wandered toward the Pennsylvania delegation. There I heard "Drop Cameron," "Defeat Seward," "Unite on Lincoln." "Perhaps get REEDER or HICKMAN [two popular Pennsylvanians] *as Vice President." I heard enough to warrant me in saying to a distinguished member of the New-York delegation that "Pennsylvania would change front on the next ballot." He shook his head and smiled so complacently that*

I was at sea again, and not knowing what to think, I kept still and didn't think at all.

[Shortly before this vote, David Davis had promised a key leader of the Pennsylvania delegation that Simon Cameron, Pennsylvania's candidate, could have a cabinet seat in a Lincoln presidency in exchange for Pennsylvania's vote on the second ballot.]

REGULAR REPORT OF THE PROCEEDINGS – continued.

Second Ballot

The second ballot was then taken.

Mr. Cameron's name was withdrawn.

For Mr. Lincoln.

New-Hampshire	9	Delaware	6
Vermont	10	Kentucky	9
Rhode Island	3	Ohio	14
Pennsylvania	48	Iowa	5

The whole vote for Lincoln was 181.

[This report of the tally left out several key state votes for Lincoln: 22 from Illinois, 26 from Indiana, 14 from Virginia, so on. The total of 181 is correct.]

For Mr. Seward.

Massachusetts	22	Kentucky	7
New-Jersey	4	Texas	6
Pennsylvania	2 1/2	Nebraska	3

The whole vote for Mr. Seward was 184 1/2

[As with Lincoln's, the tally for Seward leaves out several key individual states: 70 from New York, 12 from Michigan, 10 from Maine, 8 from Virginia, so on. The total of 184 ½ is correct.]

Bates 35		Cameron 2	
McLean 8		Dayton 10	
Chase 42 1/2		Cassius M. Clay 2	

From Joe Howard Jr. of <u>The New-York Times</u>:

The call of the [second ballot] roll proceeded – "Pennsylvania, 2 ½ Seward, 1 Cameron, 2 ½ McLean and 48 for Abram Lincoln," was the announcement from the Chairman of that delegation, and then I knew that Lincoln was nominated ....

REGULAR REPORT OF THE PROCEEDINGS – continued.

Third ballot

The third ballot was taken amid excitement; and cries for "the ballot." Intense feeling existed during the ballot, each vote being awarded in breathless silence and expectancy.

For Mr. Lincoln.

Massachusetts 8	Maryland 9
Rhode Island 5	Kentucky 13
New-Jersey 8	Ohio (Applause) 29
Pennsylvania 52	Oregon 14

This gave Lincoln 231 ½ votes, or within 1 1/2 of a nomination.

[This telegraphed tally of the Third Ballot vote for Lincoln again leaves out several states, though the total of 231 ½ is correct. Seward still held on to 180 votes, including all 70 from New York. Bates had 22, and Chase 24 ½.]

From P. Orman Ray, 1916 address to the Chicago Historical Society.

"As the contest narrowed down, the crowd became silent. Most of the delegates and many spectators had tally sheets in order to keep track of the balloting as it progressed. When the roll of the states [on the Third ballot] *had been called and every state had voted, the ballot stood Seward 180, a loss of four and a half, while Lincoln had 231 ½, and lacked only* one and a half *of the number necessary to nominate. While these totals were being footed up, a profound stillness suddenly fell upon the Wigwam; the men ceased to talk and the ladies to flutter their fans; one could distinctly hear the scratching of pencils and the ticking of telegraph instruments on the reporters tables.*

REGULAR REPORT OF THE PROCEEDINGS – continued.

Mr. Andrew of Massachusetts then rose and corrected the vote of Massachusetts, by changing four votes, and giving them to

Lincoln, this nominating him by 2½ majority.

This, too, was a reporting error by the _Tribune_ in its telegraphed report. Publisher Horace Greeley explained the error in a signed editorial on May 22: "*... it was not till after the roll had been called through that Mr. Carter of Ohio (not Mr. Andrew of Mass., as the telegraph reported) rose and changed the four votes to Lincoln which gave him a majority of the whole number.*

Thirty years later, _Chicago Tribune_ publisher Joseph Medill, a strong Lincoln ally, would take credit for this final step, telling the *Saturday Evening Post* (August 5, 1899) that he was standing with the Ohio delegation on the convention floor next to Carter at that moment and told him "[Ohio Senator Salmon P.] Chase could have anything he wants" if Ohio put Lincoln over the top to seal the nomination, prompting Carter to switch the four votes.

REGULAR REPORT OF THE PROCEEDINGS – continued.

The Convention immediately became wildly excited.

A large portion of the delegates, who kept still, at once said the struggle was decided, and half the convention rose, cheering, shouting, and waving hats.

The audience took up cheers, and the commotion became deafening.

State after State rose, striving to change their votes to the winning candidate, but the noise and enthusiasm rendered it impossible for the delegates to make themselves heard.

Mr. McCrillis of Maine, making himself heard, said that the young giant of the West, is now of age. Maine now casts for him her 14 votes.

Mr. Andrew of Massachusetts changed the vote of the State, giving 18 to Mr. Lincoln and 8 to Mr. Seward.

Intelligence of the nomination was now conveyed to the men on the roof of the building, who immediately made the outside multitude aware of the result. The first roar of the cannon, soon mingled itself with the cheers of the people, and the same moment a man appeared in the hall bringing a large painting of Mr. Lincoln. The scene at the time beggars description; 11,000 people inside and 20,000 or 20,500 outside were yelling and shouting at once. Two cannon sent forth roar after roar in quick succession. Delegates bore up the sticks and boards bearing the names of the several States and waved them aloft over their heads, and the vast multitude before the platform were waiving hats and handkerchiefs. The whole scene was one of the wildest enthusiasm.

Wm. M. Evarts, of New-York, having obtained a hearing, said: "Mr. Chairman, can New-York have the silence of the Convention? [Cries, yes; yes.] I ask if the vote has yet been announced. [Cries Not yet.] Then, sir, I wait to be in order."

Mr. Brown, of Missouri, desired to change 18 votes of Missouri for the gallant son of the West, Abraham Lincoln. Iowa, Connecticut, Kentucky, and Minnesota also changed their votes. The result of the third ballot was announced:

Whole number of votes cast 465

Necessary to a choice 233

Mr. Abraham Lincoln received 354, and was declared duly nominated.

The States still voting for Seward were Massachusetts, 18; New-York, 70; New-Jersey 5; Pennsylvania, ½; Maryland, 2; Michigan, 12; Wisconsin, 10; California, 3 – total, 120½.

Mr. Dayton received one vote from New-Jersey and Mr. McLean half a vote from Pennsylvania.

The result was received with renewed applause.

Concession.

When silence was restored, Wm. M. Evarts came forward on the Secretary's table and spoke as follows:

Mr. Chairman, Gentlemen of the National Convention: The State of New-York, by full delegation, with complete unanimity in purpose at home, came to the Convention and presented one of its citizens, who had served the State from childhood up, and labored for it and loved. We came here, a great State, with, as we thought, a great statesman [applause]; and our love of the great Republic from *which we are all Delegates. ... Gentlemen, it was from Gov. Seward that most of us learned to love Republican principles and the Republican party. [Cheers.] His fidelity to the country, the Constitution, and the laws, his fidelity to the party and the principles that majorities govern, his interest in the advancement of our party to its victory that our country may rise to its true glory, Reduces me to declare that I speak his sentiments, as I do the united opinion of our delegation when I move, Sir, as I do now, that the nomination of Abraham Lincoln of Illinois as the Republican candidate for the suffrages of the whole country for the office of Chief Magistrate of the American union be made unanimous. [Applause, and three cheers for New-York.]*

From Joe Howard Jr. of <u>The New-York Times</u>:

The various states changed their votes so that, with the exception of New-York, all voted for Lincoln. Mr. Evarts claimed the floor. Mounting a table, with grief manifest in his countenance, his hands clenched nervously, and every nerve quivering with excitement, he delivered one of the most interesting and able speeches I have ever heard from him or anyone else. As he feelingly and affectionately described his friend and leader, detailing his efforts in the cause of the Republican Party, and claiming for him the credit which is so eminently the due of Mr. Seward, the spectator could not fail to be impressed with the idea that a man who could have such a friend must be a noble man indeed, and that this token of unswerving devotion to principle and friendship was preeminently honorable in the eloquent speaker. In conclusion, he moved that the nomination be made unanimous. This was carried, and after some delay the Chair announced feebly and not with much spirit, that Abram Lincoln was the choice of the Convention for their candidate for the office of President of the united states of America.

I have described one

SCENE OF APLAUSE

and cannot described another. It was like the first, only more so. A huge cannon was wheeled up to the door, and bang it went every half minute for seventeen minutes steady. Some one brought in a large crayon portrait of Mr. Lincoln and carried it like the Host, up and down the platform. The Illinois, Indiana, and Ohio delegates seemed wild. They acted like madmen. One smashed his hat on another's head, who returned the compliment, which was followed by a mutual embrace. Henry G. Lane teetered up and down on a chair, not saying a word, but grinning all over his expressive countenance, while he waved in a huge circumference a pole, damaged somewhat from its frequent contact with the head of a fellow delegate. At every discharge of the cannon, the cheering would break out anew, and the wildest confusion reigned, which occasionally would reach such a pitch as to send the blood tingling through one, and stir up the fountains of his sympathies as the storm arouses the seas of the great deep.

No human body could attend to business after such scene,

and the Convention adjourned to 5 o'clock this afternoon.

REGULAR REPORT OF THE PROCEEDINGS – continued.

A life-size portrait of Abraham Lincoln was there exhibited from the platform amid renewed cheers.

Mr. Andrews of Massachusetts on the part of the united delegation of that State, seconded the motion of the gentleman of New-York, that the nomination be made unanimous. After declaring the devotion of Massachusetts to the principle of freedom and equality, he extolled Gov. Seward as a statesman and patriot, and pledged the State to roll up over 100,000 majority and give its 18 electoral votes to the candidates.

Eloquent speeches, endorsing the nominee, were also made by Carl Schurz, F. P. Blair of Missouri, and Mr. Browning of Illinois, all of which breathed a spirit of confidence and enthusiasm.

At the close, three hearty cheers were given for New-York, and the nomination of Mr. Lincoln made unanimous.

With loud cheers for Lincoln, the Convention adjourned till 5 o'clock.

From Joe Howard Jr. of *The New-York Times*:

Since the adjournment, there has been a grand Lincoln

demonstration – a Lincoln mass-meeting and serenades without number. The rooms of the Massachusetts Delegation are directly opposite mine, and Gilmore's band is now in there playing "When Swallows Homeward Fly." The rooms of the Pennsylvania Delegation are "round the corner," and the Pittsburgh band strokes up "Hail Columbia," after which the "Light-guard band" of Chicago, which is stationed in the hall below, gives us the benefit of the "Star Spangled Banner"; so you see we have pretty lively times, and all that quiet which is so desirable when a man is sleepy and tagged out as I am, or when he has a letter to be written and mailed in half-an-hour as I have. The halls are filled with politicians, all laboring for an end. Everybody has been or is drinking, but I have not seen a drunken person since my coming here. Though there is great confusion and a great deal of loud talk, there is no ill-nature visible and no single row has occurred since the Convention sat.

I should be glad to continue, but for three good reasons I must close:

1. The mail closes in five minutes.

2. Convention meets in twenty minutes.

3. I am physically exhausted.

As old Plumb Gut used to say, when he wrote those tearfully and wonderfully made Republican leaders in 1856, "That'sall."

--Howard

P.S. It will be too late for me to send anything by this mail. The particulars of the nomination will be sent by telegraph and you

will have written half a dozen articles thereon before this reaches
you. Nevertheless, I shall for my own individual fun, take the liberty
of guessing, and recording a bet made just now, that the ticket will
be either Lincoln and Hickman or Lincoln and Banks. [Howard
was wrong on both of his predictions. The ticket would be
Lincoln and Hannibal Hamlin.]

8. DAY THREE – FOR VICE PRESIDENT

Lincoln and his team stated no preference over the party's nominee for Vice President. Instead, they left the choice to the Convention delegates. The result was a three-way contest between (a) Maine's former Governor and U.S. Senator Hannibal Hamlin, (b) Kentuckian Cassius M. Clay, and (c) Pennsylvania Congressman John Hickman

From the _New York Tribune_, May 19, 1860.

REGULAR REPORT OF THE PROCEEDINGS – continued.

Chicago, Friday, May 18, 1860.

The Convention reassembled at 5 o'clock.

A large banner was brought on the platform by Pennsylvania, bearing the inscription, "Pennsylvania good for 20,000 majority for the People's Candidate, Abe Lincoln." It was received with loud applause.

At 5½ o'clock order was obtained, and the PRESIDENT announced the business before the Convention to be a ballot for Vice-

President.

Mr. Vilder of Kansas Named John Hickman of Pennsylvania.

Mr. Lewis of Pennsylvania seconded the nomination. [Applause.]

Mr. Carter of Ohio named Hannibal Hamlin of Maine.

Mr. Boutwell of Massachusetts named N. P. Banks of Massachusetts. [Loud applause.]

Mr. Smith of Indiana named Cassius M. Clay. [Loud applause.]

Mr. Lowry of Pennsylvania named Gov. Reeder of Pennsylvania.

A ballot was then taken, with the following results.

For Hannibal Hamlin.

Maine	16	Ohio	46
New-Hampshire	10	Indiana	8
Vermont	10	Michigan	8
Massachusetts	1	Illinois	2
Rhode Island	8	Wisconsin	3
Connecticut	5	Iowa	6
New-York	35	Minnesota	6
Pennsylvania	11	Oregon	1
Maryland	8		
Delaware	2	Total	194

For Cassius M. Clay.

Connecticut	3	Michigan	4
New-York	9	Illinois	2
New-Jersey	1	Wisconsin	5
Pennsylvania	4½	Minnesota	1
Maryland	2	Nebraska	1
Delaware	3	District of Columbia	2
Virginia	23		
Kentucky	23	Total	101½
Indiana	18		

For John Hickman. [A congressman from Pennsylvania.]

Massachusetts	1	California	8
Connecticut	8	Minnesota	1
New-York	11	Oregon	3
Pennsylvania	7	Kansas	6
Maryland	1	Nebraska	9
Delaware	1		
Missouri	9	Total	58
Illinois	2		

For Gov. Reeder – Massachusetts, 1; New-York, 2; New-Jersey, 7; Pennsylvania, 24; Illinois, 16; Iowa, 1. Total, 51.

For N. P. Banks – Massachusetts, 20; Connecticut, 1; New-York, 4; Pennsylvania, 2½; Missouri, 9; Iowa, 1; Oregon, 1. Total, 38½.

For Henry Winter Davis – New-York, 8.

For Sam Houston – Texas, 6. [Houston had also received votes for President at the May 9 convention of the Constitutional Union Party in Baltimore, but lost that nomination to John Bell.]

For Wm. L. Dayton – 3.

For Mr. Read of Pennsylvania – 1.

Total 461. Necessary to a choice, 232.

Second Ballot

The second ballot was then taken.

Massachusetts withdrew the name of Mr. Banks, and cast 26 votes for Mr. Hamlin.

Pennsylvania withdrew the name of Gov. Reeder, and cast 54 votes for Mr. Hamlin.

New-York cast 70 votes for Mr. Hamlin.

The result of the vote was announced as follows:

Hamlin 367   Clay 86

Hickman 13

The result was received with tumultuous applause.

When order was restored, Mr. Blakely of Kentucky said:

Mr. CHAIRMAN: On behalf of that gallant son of freedom, Cassius M. Clay, and his friends, I move that the nomination be made unanimous; and in retiring from the Convention, at the close of the proceedings, allow me to tender to you, on the part of the friends of Mr. Clay, our thanks for your liberal support.   In presenting his name to you, we presented the name of one who rolls the end of freedom under his tongue, while on his lips sweet liberty loves to linger. [Laughter and applause.]

Mr. Smith of Indiana seconded the motion, and made an eloquent speech in support of the nomination and in enology of Wm. H. Seward.

Mr. McCrillis of Maine, on the part of the people of Maine, expressed thanks for the honor done the State by the nomination, and declared that Maine would cast her vote for Lincoln, Hamlin, Union and victory.....

Amos Tuck of New-Hampshire moved that the President of the Convention and Chairmen of the several delegations be a Committee to inform Messrs. Lincoln and Hamlin of their nomination. Adopted.

Resolutions

.... Mr. Allen of Indiana took the floor, and made an eloquent speech in favor of the whole ticket, and pledged Indiana for 10,000 majority, and his honor for the redemption of the pledge.

Loud cries were here made for Greeley, which were met by applause and hisses.

Mr. Goodrich of Minnesota announced that a triumphal procession would parade the streets to-night, and march to the Wigwam, where a grand ratification meeting would be held. [Loud cheers.] Mr. Goodrich moved a vote of thanks to the ladies and gentlemen of Chicago for the liberality displayed in building and decorating the Wigwam. Carried unanimously.

The Convention accepted the invitation of the Rock Island

and Chicago and Galena Railroads for excursion rides on their roads.

Mr. Ashley of Ohio moved the following:

Resolved, That the Republican National Committee appointed by this Convention be and they are hereby instructed to prescribe uniform rules, that shall operate equally in all the States and Territories, whereby in the future the wishes and preferences of the electors in the Republican organization in the choice of candidates for President and Vice-President may be fully and fairly ascertained, ...

After some skirmishing, laid on the table.

Mr. Washburn of Vermont moved a vote of thanks of the Convention to the President for the ability and courtesy with which he discharged the duties of this office. Carried unanimously.

A vote of thanks was also passed to the other officers of the Convention, especially the Recording Secretary, Prait of Indiana.

The following was announced as the National Committee for the next four years, Pennsylvania alone unfilled:

Maine . . . . .C. J. Gillman
Kentucky. . . . . .C.M. Clay
New-Hampshire . . . . . .G.G. Fogg
Ohio. . . . . Thos. Spoon
Vermont. . . . . .L. Brainard
Indiana. . . . . S. Meredith
Massachusetts . . . . . . .J.Z. Goodrich
Missouri. . . . . Alan S. Jones
Rhode Island . . . . Thos. G. Turner
Michigan. . . . . Austin Blair
Connecticut. . . . . Gideon Wells

Illinois. . . . .   N.B. Judd
New-York. . . . .   Edwin D. Morgan
Texas. . . . .   D. Henderson
New-Jersey. . . . .   Downing Duer
Wisconsin. . . . .   Carl Schulz
Maryland. . . . .   Jas. F. Waggoner
Iowa. . . . .   A.J. Stevens
Delaware. . . . . .N.B. Smithers
California. . . . .   D.W. Cheeseman
Virginia. . . . .   Alfred Caldwell

The convention then adjourned.

Special Dispatch to the *New York Tribune*.

CHICAGO, Friday, May 18-8 ½ p.m. ....   *There is a very general satisfaction with the ticket. New-York is bitterly disappointed, but promises to go in heartily. The West is in a high state of jubilation. Col. Lane says Indiana is now sure both in October and November. Dispatches from Pennsylvania announce a most enthusiastic reception. A Bell man presides over a Philadelphia ratification meeting tonight.*

Mr. Lincoln's romantic personal history, his eloquence as an orator, and his firm personal integrity, give augury of a successful campaign – one of the 1810 stamp.

Most of the Eastern delegates make excursions to different parts of the West before returning. Most of the Massachusetts delegation visit the Capital of Wisconsin by invitation of the

Governor. The Railroad Company are granting free tickets liberally, and some are making up special excursion trains.

11:30 P.M. – Chicago is in a blaze of glory tonight. Bonfires, processions, torchlights, fireworks, illuminations, and salutes, have filled the air with noise and the eye with beauty. "Honest Old Abe" is the cry in every mouth, and the "irrepressible conflict" against Slavery and corruptions opens with great promise and immense enthusiasm. It is impossible to exaggerate the good feeling and joy that prevail here. The Illinois delegation resolved that the millennium has come. The Wigwam is packed with people, and Messrs. Giddings, Curtin of Pennsylvania, Wyman of Boston, and others, made rousing speeches.

Dispatches from the interior report everywhere the greatest enthusiasm – bonfires, salutes, and the highest joy.

Some of the Illinois delegation fairly cried with happiness at the success of "Old Abe." They say it is a triumph of the people over politicians.

9. REACTIONS:

Within seconds of the final Convention votes, telegraph wires flashed the news across the country, resulting in celebrations and some grumbling. Without public opinion polls, these events were still the best way to gauge public reaction to the nominations.

From the _New York Tribune_, May 19, 1860.

At Albany.

ALBANY, Friday, May 18, 1860.

One hundred guns are now being fired by some of the enthusiastic Republicans of this city in honor of the nomination of Lincoln for President. The greatest excitement prevails in the city. The streets are alive with politicians, and groups are gathered on State street and Broadway, discussing the subject of the nomination. The announcement of the nomination was entirely unexpected by the Republicans of this city. They were confident that Wm. H. Seward was to be the man, and when it was announced that Lincoln was the nominee, a feeling of disappointment was manifest. At first the *intelligence was not credited, but these doubts were of short duration. This feeling still exists, but they say that they will abide by the decision of the Convention; and give Lincoln a hearty and cordial support.*

AT ROCHESTER.

ROCHESTER, Friday, May 18, 1860.

A salute of 100 guns was fired this afternoon by the Republicans in favor of the nomination of Abraham Lincoln.

AT PHILADELPHIA.

PHILADELPHIA, Friday, May 18, 1860.

An enthusiastic ratification meeting was held at the Republican Headquarters to-night. A grand torch light procession is now marching the streets. The nomination of Lincoln is received with favor among the party throughout the State, it being the work of the Pennsylvania delegation.

AT WASHINGTON.

WASHINGTON, Friday, May 18, 1860.

Mr. Hamlin's rooms are crowded to-night with friends congratulating him on his nomination. He had no expectation of receiving it, and was surprised when it was announced to him. The Republicans of this city and the Republican Congressmen are full of enthusiasm over the ticket.

AT DETROIT.

DETROIT, Friday, May 18, 1860

A salute of 100 guns was fired here this afternoon, and bonfires and illuminations were the order of the evening, in honor of the nomination of Lincoln and Hamlin.

AT BUFFALO.

BUFFALO, Friday, May 18, 1860.

A salute was fired here this afternoon upon the receipt of the news of the nomination of Lincoln and Hamlin. No other evidences of mad enthusiasm, however, were witnessed.

AT BANGOR.

BANGOR, Friday, May 16, 1860.

One hundred guns were fired, and the Republicans are jubilant for the Chicago nominations.....

AT BOSTON.

BOSTON, Friday, May 18, 1860.

Mr. Lincoln's nomination for President caused some surprise, but was well received generally by the Republicans, who hailed the announcement with a salute of 100 guns.

It is proposed to have a grand Ratification Meeting at Faneuil Hall on Monday night.

AT CONCORD.

CONCORD, N.H., Friday, May 18, 1860.

The Republicans of this city received Mr. Lincoln's nomination with great enthusiasm. A salute of 100 guns was fired, and bonfires lighted this evening.

AT BATH.

BATH, Me., Friday, May 18, 1860.

A salute of 100 guns, fireworks, ringing of bells, and a street procession with music, inaugurates the Republican campaign in this city.

AT PORTLAND.

PORTLAND, Friday, May 18, 1860.

The Chicago nominations were received with great enthusiasm. A salute of 100 guns, bonfires, etc.

IN NEW YORK CITY.

... At first there was considerable disappointment at the result. Seward's chances were considered to be so strong that his nomination was deemed a forgone conclusion. When the news of Lincoln's nomination came, it was taken to be a hoax, and not a few persons insisted that it was so, until the publication of the evening edition of The TRIBUNE dissipated all doubt, by fully confirming *the intelligence.*

Then there was a curious exhibition of feeling. The more ultra Republicans sadly regretted the defeat of Mr. Seward...

With very few exceptions, the live, working Republicans of the city hailed the nomination with hearty satisfaction. Within an hour after the news arrived, every public place and every street corner had its crowd interested in this theme only. The distress of the Democracy was the best evidence of the strength of the nomination. Oh, how sorry they were for Mr. Seward! A stranger might have been excused for believing that Mr. S. was the ideal of the Democratic party, instead of being the most radical of all the statesmen of the other side.

Of course a noise must be made, and two six-pounders were brought to the Park, and fired each a hundred times – one of them by order of the Republican General Committee, and the other under the patronage of private citizens. Beside these, the Central Committee ordered one hundred guns to be fired in Madison and Hamilton squares respectively. In Mount Morris square [today's Marcus Garvey Park, at 117th street between 6th and 7th Avenues], *also, the big gun was brought out, and a hundred rounds announced to the citizens the nomination of Lincoln and Hamlin. Great numbers of enthusiastic Republicans gathered in the square, and the excitement was intense....*

The Douglas men bluster bravely. They say that their man will now certainly be nominated, and that he will carry Illinois,

New-York, Pennsylvania, New-Jersey, Connecticut, and perhaps New-Hampshire – thus throwing the election into the House – that is, unless the South go for Douglas; which they do not consider possible....

THE TRIBUNE office was crowded all the afternoon, and opinions were very freely expressed. There were some personal regrets expressed, but "Honest old Abe" was fully indorsed by the people....

There was a pretty general wish expressed that John Hickman or Winter Davis should be on for Vice President, and Hamlin's name was not so enthusiastically received as that of Lincoln.

View of a Seward supporter:

Signed editorial in the *Albany Evening Journal* by "G.D." [George Dawson], a co-publisher of the paper along with Thurlow Weed.

Mr. Seward's Defeat

CHICAGO, May 19, 1880.
Misrepresentation has achieved its work. The timid and credulous have succumbed to threats and perversions. To please a few thousand men of equivocal principle and faltering faith, millions of loyal hearts have been saddened. The recognized standard-bearer of the Republican party has been sacrificed upon the altar of fancied

availability.

This sacrifice was alike cruel and unnecessary. No man in the Republican party has greater strength than WILLIAM H. SEWARD. No man deserves more at the hands of that party, or possesses greater fitness for the high office for which its national tribunal has declared him unworthy.... He, more than any other man, initiated the principles which called it into being, and which gave and which still gives the Republican party all its vitality. No other man's history so distinctly embodies the grand idea which brought together those who originally entered into the Republican organization; and the world's verdict was that good faith, common honesty and the future history and well-being of the Republican Party demanded his nomination as its standard-bearer in the pending canvass.

He was deemed too pure, too consistent, too heroic, too wise, and too thoroughly and too conspicuously imbued with the distinctive principles of Republicanism, to succeed.

Men, no single pulsation of whose heart ever beat responsive to the principles of the Republican party, must be conciliated; and, to do so WILLIAM H. SEWARD must be sacrificed. Localities where Republicanism never had vitality enough to breathe, were coveted; and to encourage the party to achieve what is un attainable, WILLIAM H. SEWARD was sacrificed. States, whose representatives have never yet inhaled sufficient of the free spirit of Republicanism, to assume its name, demanded the immolation, and they were gratified....

The result is less a defeat of WILLIAM H. SEWARD than a triumph of his personal enemies. The sentiment which culminated in his rejection was chiefly manufactured by those whose dislike of the man was infinitely in advance of their love of his principles. For years he has been their Mordecai at the King's gate; and by feeding the doubts of some, by exciting the apprehensions of others, and by the industrious utterance of misrepresentations to all, they have like their ancient prototype, seemingly attained the end they have so ardently coveted,... I know, very well, that many of those by whose hands this immolation was actually consummated, did not share in this spirit of envy and hate; but enough did to turn the scale.

--But for none of this work of credulity, in gratitude and malignity, is ABRAHAM LINCOLN, or his immediate friends, responsible. Those who were most zealous in their malign labors, and most industrious and effective in their studied perversions, had no love for the successful candidate. He was neither their first nor their second choice. Others were preferred and pressed before him; but it was because those others were less imbued with the pure principles of Republicanism, and were deemed more offensive to Mr. SEWARD'S friends, than because those to whom I refer were not willing to accept Mr. LINCOLN or any other man, as an instrument for the accomplishment of their primary purpose. Mr. LINCOLN is a bold, gallant and uncompromising Republican.

He, however, owes nothing to Mr. SEWARD'S immediate

friends. They labored earnestly to prevent his nomination. They deemed him greatly the inferior, in every way, of their candidate. And they said so, kindly but with emphasis. ... The men and influences which secured Mr. LINCOLN's nomination, may not, all of them, labor with equal zeal and effectiveness, to secure his election. But upon them devolves the responsibility of the campaign; and, if successful, as we hope, in the battle upon them will devolve, also, the direction, management and success of the administration which the election will initiate. Mr. SEWARD'S friends will take places in the ranks of the party, which have been assigned them; and, so soon as time shall have soothed the wounds which the Convention has inflicted, they will be found, as in every battle which has yet been fought for Freedom, doing yeoman's service.

--In all that I have thus written, I desire the readers of the Journal to hold me individually and alone responsible. Although with him at Chicago after the nomination was made, I had no heart to seek advice from, or in any way to counsel with, Mr. [Thurlow] WEED, I believe he will deem some things I have here written ill-timed and injudicious. But I have neither his forbearance, sagacity nor discretion. In this epistle, therefore, I speak my own sentiments, regardless of what my associates may think or say, and quite indifferent as to all consequences personal to myself. My chief regret is, that there is any justification for what I have said, and that hundreds of thousands of true Republicans have already thought all and more than I have written. G. D. [George Dawson]

Stephen Douglas's reaction:

Special Dispatch to the _New York Tribune_.

WASHINGTON, Friday, May 18, 1860.

.... _About 2 o'clock Mr. Haskin telegraphed Mr. Douglas that Mr. Lincoln was nominated, but the fact was discredited in consequence of several bogus dispatches having been circulated, even though one of the operators testified to its genuineness. An hour and a half elapsed before any confirmation was obtained, and then telegrams announcing the result multiplied rapidly. ...._

Mr. Douglas spoke of [Lincoln] _in the presence of Republicans and Democrats as an upright, gifted, and popular candidate, who had great strength in the North-West, and would carry Illinois against any other candidate but himself, by 20,000._

_... Mr._ [Georgia United States Senator Robert A.] _Toombs and others who were heretofore well-disposed toward Mr. Douglas, consider this nomination as disposing of him effectually, because his main pretension in the Free States rested upon his alleged strength in the North-West, which is now completely extinguished. On this score there is hardly a difference of opinion, because the States which preferred either Mr. Seward or Mr. Bates in that section, concur through their representatives here in the belief that Mr. Lincoln will call out a larger vote than either._

William Seward's reaction:

Letter from William H. Seward to Thurlow Weed
May 18, 1860. Auburn, New York.   From Memoirs of Thurlow Weed.

My Dear Weed--

You have my unbounded gratitude for this last as for a whole life of efforts in my behalf.

I wish that I were sure that your sense of disappointment is as light as my own. It ought to be equally so, if we have been equally thoughtful and zealous for friends, party, and country. I know not what has been left undone that could have been done, or done that ought to be regretted.

You see that I am not expecting you to stop here on your way home, although Mrs. Seward and I have hoped that Harriet might stay with us a day or two.

Ever faithfully yours,   William H. Seward

10. INFORMING THE NOMINEE

Two days after the convention, a delegation chosen by the Convention travelled from Chicago to Springfield, Illinois, to meet Abraham Lincoln and notify him formally of his nomination as President of the United States.

MR. LINCOLN AT HOME: Visit of the Official Delegation.

From the *Chicago Press and Tribune;*

Springfield, May 19, 1860

The special train generously provided by the managers of the Illinois Central Railroad for the conveyance to Springfield of the gentlemen - chairman of the State delegations headed by the President of the Convention, Hon. Geo. Ashmun - charged by the Convention with the duty of officially informing Mr. LINCOLN of his nomination, left the depot at the foot of Lake street, and reached Urbana without accident and hardly without a stop. Here a delay of a few minutes occurred, during which the airs of the Philadelphia Cornet Band, which the Pennsylvanians had engaged for the occasion, called together a crowd of people from the stores, gardens and shops within ear-shot of the station, and they, learning what was the object of the excursion, soon added their long, loud, and enthusiastic shouts for Honest Old Abe, to the sound of the music – music and shouts all in honor of the glorious nominations which had been made.

The crowd was irrepressible and would be content with nothing less than a speech. In a few brief, pertinent and enthusiastic remarks, by Governor Morgan of New York, Hon. Mr. Carter of Ohio, Judge Kelly of Pennsylvania, Carl Schurz of Wisconsin, and one or two others, the good feeling of the crowd and the zeal of the speakers were wrought up.

At Decatur, just struck with news of the approaching train, a large crowd of people were on the platform, and there, as at Urbana; the delegation was received with round after round of hearty applause. Dave Cartter, who had, by general approbation, been chosen orator for the occasion, was seized by the enthusiastic people, mounted on a temporary rostrum, and forced to discourse of the happiness of the nominations and the certainty of a Republican triumph.....

At Springfield, almost the whole population were at the depot, and as the train approached, firing of cannon, strains of martial music, and hurrahs of the multitude signalized the popular approbation of tile errand on which the delegation had come. With difficulty, owing to the rush, a procession was formed and took up the line of march for the Chenery House, where the liberality of the citizens had laid out ample refreshments for the party. The scene in the streets was an ovation of which any private citizen might be proud. The tribute of neighbors with whom our candidate had lived on terms of great personality for years-a tribute in which there was no sign of envy or jealousy-it was doubly gratifying. In the evening, the delegation, accompanied by forty or fifty outsiders, walked up to Mr. Lincoln's house and were at once ushered into his presence. The parlors of his residence, small but neatly and tastefully furnished, were thrown together by the opening of the folding doors, and he stood at the bottom or the back parlor, gracefully bowed as the delegates entered, and after a moment's delay motioned Mr. Ashmun to proceed. In a peculiarly appropriate speech, which you have already published, delivered in a tone of voice and with the subdued earnestness of manner appropriate to the occasion, that gentleman discharged his duty.

> "I have, sir, the honor in behalf of the gentlemen who are present, a committee appointed by the Republican convention recently assembled at Chicago, to discharge a most pleasant duty. We have come, sir, under a vote of instructions to notify you that you have been selected by the convention of Republicans at Chicago, as their candidate for President of the United States. ...I desire to present you the letter which has been prepared and which informs you of the nomination and with it the platform, reports and sentiments which the Convention adopted. Sir, at your convenience we shall be glad to receive from you such a response as It may be your pleasure to give us."

Of course all eyes were upon the man who now occupies so large a share of the thoughts and so warm a place in the hopes of the American people. He stood the test of scrutiny. Without other evidence of emotion than that seen in an unnatural paleness and a compressed lip, be stepped forward at the conclusion of Mr. Ashmun's short address, and with a voice as clear us a bell, in natural tones and with slow and distinct utterances, pronounced his reply.

Men who had taken up the notion from Mr. Lincoln's soubriquet, *that he was a rough diamond, who would not shine in the White House, that he was a stump orator only, popular with the masses but unused to occasions which require tact and polite address, were astonished by his manifestations of ease and grace; and when the gentlemen present were introduced by name, there was not one who did not the more cordially grasp the honest man's hand because of the agreeable surprise to which they bad been treated.*

> *"Mr. Chairman, and Gentlemen of the Committee, I tender you, and through you, to the Republican National Convention, and all the people represented in it, my profoundest thanks for the high honor done me, which you formally announce. Deeply and even painfully sensible of the great responsibility which is inseparable from that honor — a responsibility which I could almost wish had fallen upon some one of the far more eminent men and experienced Statesmen whose distinguished names were before the Convention, I shall, by your leave, consider more fully the resolutions of the Convention, denominated the Platform, and without unreasonable delay, respond to you, Mr. Chairman, in writing, not doubting that the Platform will be found satisfactory, and the nomination accepted; and now I will no longer defer the pleasure of taking you and each of you by the hand."*

In their minds the fear that the man who had mauled rails, driven oxen, and tugged at the flat-boat oar, could not have that polish which the etiquette of the salon requires, fell dead forever. They were the more pleased because his politeness had the charm of sincerity and naturalness. Frank Pierce [former President Franklin Pierce], *of all men in America, is the best at the French bow, and is good for nothing else.* Mr. Buchanan [then-President James Buchanan] *is said to have a courtly ease that makes its way in all crowds; but we doubt if either could have impressed the gentlemen before us as Mr. Lincoln did, by the manifestation of the kindly qualities of his nature.*

The ceremonies being concluded, the gentlemen passed in groups to another parlor on the right of the hall, where they wore received by Mrs. Lincoln, with that grace and intelligence which have made her a distinguished ornament of the excellent society of the capital. The visitors were anxious not only to see tho man who will wield the power of the nation, but the woman also to whom the hospitalities and social influences of the White House will be entrusted. They were satisfied that both will be in capable hands. So much for the reception.

On the return of the party to the hotel, the enthusiasm of the citizens broke forth anew. Every Republican house around the handsome square was illuminated the State House was a blaze of light, the air was tilled with exploding rockets and the ears of all were stunned by the booming of cannon and the resonant cheers of the happy multitudes glad to do honor to their neighbor who had received as a free gift one of the highest honors that can be bestowed upon man. The people were fairly wild with delight. A meeting addressed by excellent speakers of national reputation was going on in the Representatives' Hall; but nothing but the open air and the liberty to cry out with all possible strength of lung for the nominees would satisfy the excited citizens. As long as rockets and powder were to be had and as long as there was one throat left capable of a cheer, the demonstrations were kept up.

At 12 o'clock, midnight, the delegation left on their return to Chicago, carrying with them the impression that Mr. Lincoln has the capability of gracing any position to which he may be raised, and that the love and approbation of his townsmen, so signally displayed, are evidences that no station is too exalted for his merits.

I cannot close without expressing the obligations of the party to the managers of the Illinois Central Road, particularly to CoL. Foster, of the Land Department, and his assistant, Mr. Austin, for the entire safety of the trip. Their arrangements were so complete that not a mistake or delay occurred to mar the pleasure of the occasion. Called upon to run a train out of time, and at an extraordinary speed, often as great as fifty miles an hour, they did their duty so well that no praise is too high. They were seconded by Mr. Bowen, the Superintendent of the Western Road, over a part of which the train passed. To their joint care we owe the safety and peace by which the memorable occasion was marked.   YOURS,

11. POSTSCRIPT:
INAUGURATION DAY, 1861

With the Republican nomination in hand, Abraham Lincoln faced three opponents for the presidency in 1860: Stephen A. Douglas, the Illinois U.S. Senator nominated by northern Democrats meeting in Baltimore on June 18; John C. Breckinridge, the sitting Vice President of the United States and slave-holder from Kentucky, nominated by southern Democrats, also meeting in Baltimore that June; and John Bell representing the new Constitutional Union Party.

Lincoln followed custom and spent the entire campaign at home in Springfield, Illinois, letting his friends and supporters – including former rival William H. Seward – carry the argument, speaking on his behalf across the country.

That November, Americans voted in large numbers, with fully 81.2 percent of eligible voters going to the polls. Lincoln won 1,865,908 popular votes, 39.9 percent of the total, and captured the Presidency with a clear victory in the Electoral College, winning virtually all the northern states plus California and Oregon. John Breckinridge carried nine southern states plus Maryland and Delaware; John Bell of the Constitutional Union Party carried Virginia, Tennessee, and Kentucky.

Stephen A. Douglas decided to break tradition in 1860 and launch a nationwide speaking tour to ask personally for votes. He carried only two states, Missouri and New Jersey.

By the time Lincoln arrived in Washington, D.C., to take the oath of office on March 4, 1861, the country had already split apart. Lincoln's election had prompted seven southern states to secede and form the Confederate States of America; violence would break out in April with the shelling of Fort Sumter in Charleston harbor. By the time it ended in 1865, over 600,000 Americans North and South would die in the conflict, slavery would end, and the Union would be preserved at great cost.

Still, it was a majestic moment as power transferred to the new president that day in Washington, D.C.:

From *The New-York Times*, March 5, 1861.
By Joe Howard Jr. and others.

THE NEW ADMINISTRATION
OUR WASHINGTON DISPATCHES.
WASHINGTON, Monday, March 4.

THE DAWNING OF THE DAY.

The day to which all have looked with so much anxiety and interest has come and passed. ABRAHAM LINCOLN has been inaugurated, and "all's well."

At daylight the clouds were dark and heavy with rain, threatening to dampen the enthusiasm of the occasion with unwelcome showers. A few drops fell occasionally before 8 o'clock, but not enough to lay the dust, which, under the impulse of a strong northwest wind, swept down upon the avenue from the cross streets quite unpleasantly. The weather was cool and bracing, and, on the whole, favorable to the ceremonies of the day.

MR. LINCOLN.

MR. LINCOLN rose at 5 o'clock. After an early breakfast, the Inaugural was read aloud to him by his son ROBERT, and the completing touches were added, including the beautiful and impassioned closing paragraph. MR. LINCOLN then retired from his family circle to his closet, where he prepared himself for the solemn and weighty responsibilities which he was about to assume.

Here he remained until it was time for an audience to MR.

SEWARD. *Together these statesmen conversed concerning that paragraph of the Inaugural relating to the policy of forcing obnoxious non-resident officers upon disaffected citizens.*

When MR. SEWARD departed, MR. LINCOLN closed his door upon all visitors, until Mr. Buchanan [outgoing President James Buchanan] *called for him to escort him to the Capitol.*

THE THRONG IN THE STREETS.

From early daylight the streets were thronged with people, some still carrying carpet-bags in hand, having found no quarters in which to stop.

THE NOTE OF PREPARATION.

The busy note of preparation for the parade was soon heard on every side. The New-York delegation; over two hundred strong, formed in procession on Pennsylvania avenue at 9 o'clock, and proceeded in a body to MR. SEWARD'S residence to pay their respects. ...

THE INAUGURAL PROCESSION.

It was nearly noon when MR. BUCHANAN started from the White House with the Inaugural procession, which halted before Willard's Hotel to receive the President elect. The order of march you will get from other sources, and I will only observe that the carriage containing MR. BUCHANAN and MR. LINCOLN, was a simple open brett carriage, surrounded by the President's mounted guard, in close order, as a guard of honor.

The procession, as usual, was behind-hand a little, but its order was excellent. Nothing noteworthy occurred on the route. As it ascended the Capitol Hill, towards the north gate, the company of United States Cavalry and the President's mounted guard took their positions each side of the carriage-way, and thus guarded the enclosed passage-way by which the President's party entered the north wing of the Capitol to go to the Senate Chamber.

The procession halted until the President and suite entered, and then filed through the troops aforesaid into the grounds.

On the east front, the military took their positions in the grounds in front of the platform, but the United States troops maintained their places outside until the line took up the President and party again after the ceremonies were over, to escort them back to the White House.

ARRANGEMENTS AT THE CAPITOL.

The arrangements at the Capitol were admirably designed, and executed so that everybody who was entitled to admission got in, and everybody who could not go in could see from without. The Senate Chamber was the great point of attraction, but only the favored few were admitted upon the floor, while the galleries were reserved for and occupied by a select number of ladies. The scene which transpired there was most memorable, producing a great and solemn impression upon all present.

A few moments before 12 o'clock, MR. BRECKINRIDGE came in with MR. HAMLIN upon his arm, and, together, they sat by the side of the President's desk until noon, when, assuming the

Chair, MR. BRECKINRIDGE said: .... [John Breckinridge, who had won eleven states in the presidential election that year, would remain in Washington on leaving the Vice presidency that day. He would continue to serve as a United States Senator from Kentucky until being expelled in December 1861 for supporting the South. He would then join the Confederate army as a Major General and by 1865 would rise to become the Confederate Secretary of War.]

The oath was then administered to Vice-President HAMLIN, who announced his readiness to take it in a full, firm tone. MR. BRECKINRIDGE took him by the hand, and led him to the chair, after which, crossing over to MR. SEWARD, he shook hands and extended greetings with him, and took his seat as the newly elected Senator. The Vice-President rapped to order, and addressed the Senate as follows:

....

The Senate now waited in silence for the President elect. Gradually those entitled to the floor entered. The Diplomatic Corps, in full court dress, came quite early. The Supreme Court followed, headed by the venerable Chief Justice TANEY, who looked as if he had come down from several generations, and finally the House of Representatives filed in. For at lease an hour MR. HAMLIN was acting President of the United States, but at length, a little after 1 o'clock, the doors opened, and the expected dignitaries were announced.

THE OUTGOING AND THE INCOMING.

MR. BUCHANAN and MR. LINCOLN entered, arm in arm, the former pale, sad, nervous; the latter's face slightly flushed, with compressed lips. For a few minutes, while the oath was administered to [Maryland] Senator [James A.] PEARCE, they sat in front of the President's desk. MR. BUCHANAN sighed audibly, and frequently, but whether from reflection upon the failure of his Administration, I can't say. MR. LINCOLN was grave and impassive as an Indian martyr.

APPEARANCE AT THE EAST PORTICO.

When all was ready, the party formed, and proceeded to the platform erected in front of the eastern portico. The appearance of the President elect was greeted, as he entered from the door of the rotunda, with immense cheering by many thousand citizens assembled in the grounds, filling the square and open space, and perching on every tree, fence or stone affording a convenient point from which to see or hear. In a few minutes the portico was also densely crowded with both sexes.

On the front of the steps was erected a small wooden canopy, under which were seated MR. BUCHANAN, Chief-Justice TANEY, Senators CHASE and BAKER, and the President elect, while at the left of the small table on which was placed the Inaugural, stood Col. SHELDEN, Marshal of the District, an exponent of the security which existed there for the man and the ceremonies of the hour. At the left of the canopy, sat the entire Diplomatic Corps, dressed in gorgeous attire, evidently deeply impressed with the solemnity of the occasion, and the importance of the simple ceremony about to be performed. Beyond them was the Marine band, which played several patriotic airs before and after the reading of the address. To the right of the diplomats sat in solemn dignity, in silk gowns and hats, the members of the Supreme Court. Then came Senators, members of the House, distinguished guests and fair ladies by the score, while the immediate right of the canopy was occupied by the son and Private Secretaries of MR. LINCOLN. Perched up on one side, hanging on by the railing, surrounding the statue of COLUMBUS and an Indian girl, was Senator [Louis T.] WIGFALL [of Texas], witnessing the pageant.

MR. LINCOLN INTRODUCED.

Everything being in readiness, Senator BAKER came forward and said:

"FELLOW-CITIZENS: I introduce to you ABRAHAM LINCOLN, the President elect of the United States of America."

Whereupon, MR. LINCOLN arose, walked deliberately and composedly to the table, and bent low in honor of the repeated and enthusiastic cheering of the countless host before him. Having put on his spectacles, he arranged his manuscript on the small table, keeping the paper thereon by the aid of his cane, and commenced in a clear, ringing voice, that was easily heard by those on the outer limits of the crowd, to read his first address to the people, as

President of the United States.

RECEPTION OF THE INAUGURAL.

The opening sentence, "Fellow-citizens of the United States," was the signal for prolonged applause, the good Union sentiment thereof striking a tender chord in the popular breast. Again, when, after defining certain actions to be his duty, he said, "And I shall perform it," there was a spontaneous, and uproarious manifestation of approval which continued for some moments. Every sentence which indicated firmness in the Presidential chair, and every statement of a conciliatory nature, was cheered to the echo; while his appeal to his "dissatisfied fellow-countrymen," desiring them to reflect calmly, and not hurry into false steps, was welcomed by one and all, most heartily and cordially.

The closing sentence "upset the watering pot" of many of his hearers, and at this point alone did the melodious voice of the President elect falter. [The final line of Lincoln's inaugural address was this: "I am loath to close. We are not enemies, but friends. We must not be enemies. Though passion may have strained, it must not break our bonds of affection. The mystic chords of memory, stretching from every battlefield and patriot grave to every living heart and hearthstone all over this broad land, will yet swell the chorus of the Union, when again touched, as surely they will be, by the better angels of our nature."]

Judge TANEY did not remove his eyes from MR. LINCOLN during the entire delivery, while MR. BUCHANAN, who was probably sleepy and tired, sat looking as straight as he could at the toe of his right boot. MR. DOUGLAS, who stood by the right of the railing, was apparently satisfied, as he exclaimed, sotto voce, "Good," "That's so," "no coercion," and "Good again."

THE OATH OF OFFICE.

After the delivery of the address Judge TANEY stood up, and all removed their hats, while he administered the oath to MR. LINCOLN. Speaking in a low tone the form of the oath, he signified to MR. LINCOLN, that he should repeat the words, and in a firm but modest voice, the President took the oath as prescribed by the law, while the people, who waited until they saw the final bow, tossed their hats, wiped their eyes, cheered at the top of their voices, hurrahed themselves hoarse, and had the crowd not been so very dense, they would have demonstrated in more lively ways, their joy, satisfaction and delight.

SHAKING HANDS

Judge TANEY was the first person who shook hands with MR. LINCOLN, and was followed by MR. BUCHANAN, CHASE, DOUGLAS, and a host of minor great men. A Southern gentleman, whose name I did not catch, seized him by the hand, and said, "God bless you, my dear Sir; you will save us." To which MR. LINCOLN replied, "I am very glad that what I have said causes pleasure to Southerners, because I then know they are pleased with what is right."...

GOING TO THE WHITE HOUSE

After delaying a little upon the platform, MR. LINCOLN, and MR. BUCHANAN, arm in arm, and followed by a few privileged persons, proceeded at a measured pace to the Senate Chamber, and thence to the President's Room, while the Band played "Hail Columbia" "Yankee Doodle" and "Star Spangled Banner." In a short time the procession was reformed, and in state, the President and Ex-President were conducted to the White House....

The thirty-four little girls who personated the several States of the Union, and rode in a gaily decorated car in the procession, halted at the door while they sang "Hail Columbia;" after which they were received by the President, who gave to each and all of them a hearty and good-natured salute.

After MR. LINCOLN's hand had been well shaken, the doors were closed, and the Marshals of the day were personally introduced to him. He thanked them for the admirable arrangements of the day, and congratulated them upon the successful termination of their duties.

They then retired, and the President repaired to his private apartment, somewhat overcome by the fatigue and excitement of the day, but thankful that all things had been so very pleasant, and that literally nothing had occurred to mar the perfect harmony of the occasion.

Lincoln, once president, would appoint each of his key rivals from the Republican Convention to his cabinet: Seward as Secretary of State, Simon Cameron as Secretary of War (forced to resign in January 1862 over allegations of corruption), Salmon P. Chase as Secretary of the Treasury, and Edward Bates as Attorney General. He would also reward his two principal campaign managers, appointing David Davis to a vacant seat on the United States Supreme Count in October 1862 and naming Norman Judd as American Envoy to the Kingdom of Prussia, then a choice diplomatic post.

Lincoln with his cabinet drawn from rivals at the 1860 convention: (seated, left to right) Edward Bates, William H. Seward, Salmon P. Chase, Lincoln, and (at far right) Simon Cameron.

APPENDIX – THE PLATFORM

REPUBLICAN NATIONAL PLATFORM

Adopted in Chicago, May 1860.

RESOLVED, That we, the delegated representatives of the Republican electors of the United States, in Convention assembled, in discharge of the duty we owe to our constituents and our country, unite in the following declarations:

1. That the history of the nation, during the last four years, has fully established the propriety and necessity of the organization and perpetuation of the Republican party, and that the causes which called it into existence are permanent in their nature, and now, more than ever before, demand its peaceful and constitutional triumph.

2. That the maintenance of the principles promulgated in the Declaration of Independence and embodied in the Federal Constitution, "That all men are created equal; that they are endowed by their Creator with certain inalienable rights; that among these are life, liberty, and the pursuit of happiness; that to secure these rights, governments are instituted among men, deriving their just powers from the consent of the governed," is essential to the preservation of our Republican institutions; and that the Federal Constitution, the Rights of the States, and the Union of the States, must and shall be preserved.

3. That to the Union of the States this nation owes its

unprecedented increase in population, its surprising development of material resources, its rapid augmentation of wealth, its happiness at home and its honor abroad; and we hold in abhorrence all schemes for Disunion, come from whatever source they may: And we congratulate the country that no Republican member of Congress has uttered or countenanced the threats of Disunion so often made by Democratic members without rebuke and with applause from their political associates; and we denounce those threats of Disunion, in case of a popular overthrow of their ascendency, as denying the vital principles of a free government, and as an avowal of contemplated treason, which it is the imperative duty of an indignant People sternly to rebuke and forever silence.

4. That the maintenance inviolate of the rights of the States, and especially the right of each State to order and control its own domestic institutions according to its own judgment exclusively, is essential to that balance of powers on which the perfection and endurance of our political fabric depends; and we denounce the lawless invasion by armed force of the soil of any State or Territory, no matter under what pretext, as among the gravest of crimes.

5. That the present Democratic Administration has far exceeded our worst apprehensions, in its measureless subserviency to the exactions of a sectional interest, as especially evinced in its desperate exertions to force the infamous Lecompton Constitution upon the protesting people of Kansas; in construing the personal relation between master and servant to involve an unqualified property in persons; in its attempted enforcement, everywhere, on land and sea, through the intervention of Congress and of the Federal Courts of the extreme pretensions of a purely local interest; and in its general and unvarying abuse of the power intrusted

to it by a confiding people.

6. That the people justly view with alarm the reckless extravagance which pervades every department of the Federal Government; that a return to rigid economy and accountability is indispensible to arrest the systematic plunder of the public treasury by favored partisans, while the recent startling developments of frauds and corruptions at the Federal metropolis, show that an entire change of administration is imperatively demanded.

7. That the new dogma, that the Constitution, of its own force, carries Slavery into any or all of the Territories of the United States, is a dangerous political heresy, at variance with the explicit provisions of that instrument itself, with contemporaneous exposition, and with legislative and judicial precedent; is revolutionary in its tendency, and subversive of the peace and harmony of the country.

8. That the normal condition of all the territory of the United States is that of freedom; That as our Republican fathers, when they had abolished Slavery in all our national territory, ordained that "no person should be deprived of life, liberty, or property, without due process of law," it becomes our duty, by legislation, whenever such legislation is necessary, to maintain this provision of the Constitution against all attempts to violate it; and we deny the authority of Congress, of a territorial legislature, or of any individuals, to give legal existence to Slavery in any Territory of the United States.

9. That we brand the recent re-opening of the African slave-trade, under the cover of our national flag, aided by perversions of judicial power, as a crime against humanity and a burning shame to our country and age; and we call upon Congress to take prompt and efficient measures for the total and final suppression of that execrable traffic.

10. That in the recent vetoes, by their Federal Governors, of the acts of the Legislatures of Kansas and Nebraska, prohibiting Slavery in those Territories, we find a practical illustration of the boasted Democratic principle of Non-Intervention and Popular Sovereignty, embodied in the Kansas-Nebraska bill, and a demonstration of the deception and fraud involved therein.

11. That Kansas should, of right, be immediately admitted as a State under the Constitution recently formed and adopted by her people, and accepted by the House of Representatives.

12. That, while providing revenue for the support of the General Government by duties upon imports, sound policy requires such an adjustment of these imposts as to encourage the development of the industrial interest of the whole country; and we commend that policy of national exchanges which secures to the working men liberal wages, to agriculture renumerative prices, to mechanics and manufactures an adequate reward for their skill, labor, and enterprise, and to the nation commercial prosperity and independence.

13. That we protest against any sale or alienation to others of the Public Lands held by actual settlers, and against any view of he Homestead policy which regards the settlers as paupers or suppliants for public bounty; and we demand the passage by Congress of the complete and satisfactory Homestead measure which has already passed the House.

14. That the Republican party is opposed to any change in our Naturalization Laws or any State legislation by which the rights of citizenship hitherto accorded to immigrants from foreign lands shall be abridged or impaired; and in favor of giving a full and efficient protection to the rights of all classes of citizens, whether native or naturalized, both at home and abroad.

15. That appropriations by Congress for River and Harbor improvements of a National character, required for the accommodation and security of an existing commerce, are authorized by the Constitution, and justified by the obligations of Government to protect the lives and property of its citizens.

16. That a Railroad to the Pacific Ocean is imperatively demanded by the interest of the whole country; that the Federal Government ought to render immediate and efficient aid in its construction; and that, as preliminary thereto, a daily Overland Mail should be promptly established.

17. Finally, having thus set forth our distinctive principles and views, we invite the cooperation of all citizens, however differing on other questions, who substantially agree with us in their affirmance and support.

Viral History Press LLC is a new, independent
small publishing house dedicated to making history alive,
vital, and relevant.

Our promise remains:
History zealots -- you are not alone!

Visit us at _www.ViralHistoryPress.com_.

Or visit our Blog at _www.ViralHistory.com_.